LEAD!

DALE CARNEGIE
& ASSOCIATES

LEAD!

How to Build a High-Performing Team

Published 2021 by Gildan Media LLC
aka G&D Media
www.GandDmedia.com

Copyright © 2021 by Dale Carnegie & Associates

LEAD!. Copyright ©2021 by Dale Carnegie & Associates. All rights reserved.

No part of this book may be used, reproduced or transmitted in any manner whatsoever, by any means (electronic, photocopying, recording, or otherwise), without the prior written permission of the author, except in the case of brief quotations embodied in critical articles and reviews. No liability is assumed with respect to the use of the information contained within. Although every precaution has been taken, the author and publisher assume no liability for errors or omissions. Neither is any liability assumed for damages resulting from the use of the information contained herein.

FIRST EDITION 2021

Interior design by Meghan Day Healey of Story Horse, LLC

Library of Congress Cataloging-in-Publication Data is available upon request

ISBN: 978-1-7225-1021-3

10 9 8 7 6 5 4 3 2 1

*Keep your mind open to change all the time.
Welcome it. Court it. It is only by examining
and re-examining your options and ideas
that you can progress.*
—Dale Carnegie

We would like to acknowledge the following members of the Dale Carnegie team who contributed to this book:

- Joe Hart, *President & CEO*
- Christine Buscarino, *Chief Marketing Officer*
- Dr. Greg Story, *President, DC of Tokyo*
- Mariah Suddarth, *Trainer & Marketing Manager*
- Mark Marone, Director, *Thought Leadership*
- Clark Merrill, *Carnegie Master Trainer*
- Herb Escher, *President, DC of Western New York*
- Elizabeth Haberberger, *President, DC of St. Louis*
- Joe Caridiello, *Master Trainer & Director of Training, Southeast Florida*
- Gaweed El Nakeeb, *Carnegie Master Trainer*
- Vimi Appadoo, *Master Trainer and Managing Director, Mauritius*
- Anita Zinsmeister, *Trainer & President, DC Central and Southern NJ*
- Pallavi Jha, *Chairperson & Managing Director, DC India*
- Doug Stewart, *Trainer & Sales Leader, DC of Greater North Carolina*
- Jonathan Vehar, *Operations & Innovation, DC of Greater North Carolina*

CONTENTS

FOREWORD by Joe Hart   1
HOW TO USE THIS BOOK   5
INTRODUCTION   9

PART ONE

*Unleashing Leadership in Yourself:
Improving Your Inner Leader*

1. SELF-AWARENESS   21
2. ACCOUNTABILITY   39
3. BEING OTHERS FOCUSED   63
4. BEING STRATEGIC   87

PART TWO

*Unleashing Leadership in Others:
Bringing Out the Best in People*

5. APPLY HUMAN RELATIONS PRINCIPLES	103
6. USE APPROPRIATE TOOLS AND PROCESSES	123

PART THREE

Unleashing Desired Outcomes

7. TRUST AND PERSONAL GROWTH	163
8. POSITIVE CHANGE AND ORGANIZATIONAL GROWTH	177
9. ENGAGEMENT AND AGILITY	193
10. COMMON DIRECTION AND INNOVATION	205
CONCLUSION	221
INDEX	229

FOREWORD
Let's Get R.E.A.L.

by Joe Hart, CEO of Dale Carnegie Training

Like many emerging leaders, when I was first coming into the world of business, I read *How to Win Friends and Influence People*. The classic message of putting people first is one that resonated with me personally and professionally. As I started working with the Dale Carnegie organization, ultimately becoming the CEO, I began to really understand the meaning of that message. It's not just lip service, but is the foundation of effective leadership.

Dale Carnegie understood that every single person has greatness, and our challenge as leaders is to help them find and develop it. My experience has been that people are capable of so much more than they even know. Everyone has blind spots when it comes to hidden strengths and talents, and it takes a good leader to point them out.

How does a leader do this? The answer lies in the way we interact with each other. That really defines everything.

It affects how much we can accomplish, whether or not we are happy, and whether we inspire others to see more in themselves than they already do.

At Dale Carnegie Training, our leadership mission is simple. We strive to help people see things from a different perspective—from the other person's point of view—so that they can accomplish things that they couldn't do alone.

We wanted to discover what drives the most effective leaders. What is it that allows them to motivate and inspire others to be their very best? To get the answers, we conducted research that spanned thirteen countries and involved thousands of people. What we found was really intriguing.

We discovered that there are four characteristics that drive the greatest leaders. Those characteristics form the acronym R.E.A.L.

R: Reliable
E: Empathetic
A: Aspirational
L: Learner

In other words, great leaders are seen as doing what they say they are going to do.

They're empathetic to others. Their followers aspire to be like them. And they never stop learning. That's why we are so excited to have written this book. *LEAD!* enables emerging leaders to unlock the door to their own potential, and that of the people around them.

There is one other component to great leadership, and it's at the foundation of everything else. That component is Trust.

Think about that for a moment. If we have a leader who demonstrates certain behaviors that are usually associated with empathy—such as asking how our weekend was or how our big project is moving forward—but we don't trust them, we're not going to perceive it as empathy. We'll see it as self-serving. We won't be inspired to learn from a leader we don't trust. We certainly won't want to be like them.

Trust is the underpinning of everything else, and that's what differentiates the Dale Carnegie brand from others. Dale Carnegie was himself a trustworthy man who consistently demonstrated integrity. It's those two things, integrity and being consistent in what we say and do and how we communicate, that lead to trust.

To be the person who holds the position that Dale Carnegie himself held in this organization is a great honor and a great responsibility. It's not something I take lightly, and that's why I am excited to share the Dale Carnegie message on leadership. *LEAD!* will help you see things from a different perspective—from the other person's point of viewso that you can accomplish things that you can't do alone.

Be great!
Joe Hart, CEO

HOW TO USE THIS BOOK

Across the world, from continent to continent, in classrooms and conference rooms, Dale Carnegie trainers spend countless hours sharing the timeless messages put forth by our founder Dale Carnegie. Whether they are custom designed training programs for Fortune 500 companies, or classics that are open to the public, there's something timeless about the lessons Dale Carnegie taught.

With each generation that discovers his message, the ideas adapt to meet the demands of an ever-changing world. Communicating effectively with people, motivating them to achieve, helping them discover their inner leader—these human relations concepts are as relevant for us today as they were when they were first developed.

To apply them in our tumultuous world, we need a humble willingness to learn how to adapt the timeless truths to our current reality. Leadership is a human relations exercise more than anything else. Dale Carnegie's principles stand the test of time in helping people "win friends and influence others," which is the very essence of what being a leader is all about.

For example, while running a Dale Carnegie Immersion seminar in Arizona, Instructor Kim Ewers encountered a participant who was very uncomfortable with the course material.* An IT whiz, Matt preferred technology to people, and was surprised by the strong focus of the course on interacting with people.

Kim spent some time with Matt, coaching him on the benefits of building strong relationships, and how doing so would help him to foster communication with coworkers. Upon reflection, Matt realized that although he was more comfortable with technology, he could not get his job done without interacting with people. He recognized that having positive and productive relationships with people was critical to his success, and happiness in general.

The next day, Matt returned with a changed attitude and an open mind. He went on to receive accolades from his peers, and awards in Human Relations and Breakthrough from his instructors.

Like most elegant truths, the ideas in this book are simple to understand. We don't need an MBA or to have been

---

* http://www.dalecarnegiewaynj.com/2019/04/23/stories-from-the-classroom/

a leader for our whole career. They may be simple, but they require work and effort to apply and integrate into how we act on a daily basis. If we are willing to learn and continually practice the concepts found here, then we can become better leaders.

INTRODUCTION

Blending Performance Needs with Human Needs

It was pitch black and the sound of falling rocks could still be heard. It was every miner's nightmare. In a matter of minutes that sound meant that the nightmare had become reality for thirty-four men trapped below the surface of the earth in Chile in 2010. Foreman Luis Urzua knew at that moment that the only way to keep himself and the other trapped miners alive was to rapidly develop a plan that would keep them safe until help could arrive, and provide realistic hope that they would survive despite the terrifying situation.

Within moments of the collapse, Luis gathered the men together and began formulating. They developed a three-pronged strategy with three goals in mind. Keep the men healthy and alive, create order and structure while they waited, and work with the rescuers to give them the information they needed. He knew that he needed to oversee, protect, and balance the physical, emotional, and human needs of thirty-four people, potentially for months.

To accomplish the physical goal of *sustaining life,* Luis implemented a strict food rationing system—each person received two spoonfuls of tuna and half a glass of milk every other day. This kept them alive until the rescuers were able to pass food down through a small hole drilled into the earth.

To *create order and structure,* Luis led the men to organize different living spaces underground. Using his skills as a topographer, he divided the area into a work area, a sleeping space, and other defined areas. He created an artificial "day" and "night" by using the headlights of trucks in the mine to simulate daylight.

To *keep safe*, the men worked to chip away at the "roof" so that rocks wouldn't fall on them at night. And to *assist in their rescue,* they drew sophisticated maps of the underground and passed them up to rescue workers.

In addition to tending to the physical needs of the group, he also created a "leadership team" designating men to fill roles as a medic, a chaplain, and someone to administer the medical and psychological tests being sent from the surface to monitor their mental and emotional health.

For almost two months, the men lived, worked, and celebrated the small wins achieved daily.

In the end, the men were rescued after 70 days, with Luis being the last man out. Every single person lived, and they all attributed this to Luis Urzua's emergent leadership skills.

While this example is an extreme case of life or death, the leadership lessons we can draw from it apply in many different circumstances.

None of us have been trapped in a cave for almost two months in the dark. But many of us have had the experience of hearing rumors of a merger, a "restructuring," a layoff, or closure that no one in upper management can confirm or deny. What do we do when we have a team of people looking at us for guidance, but we're "in the dark," too?

Or when our boss is suddenly let go or quits and there's a huge gap in the organizational structure. Now it's up to us to lead, even though we may not be formally in that role. It's fairly easy to be an empathetic, trustworthy leader when things are going well—but what about when they're not? When there's chaos and uncertainty, the best intentions of leaders sometimes disappear. That's true for leaders around us and for ourselves.

At its core, leadership is a way to achieve results through and with other people. The results may look different from organization to organization, and the people and methods may change, but the fundamental requirements of a leader are the same. Leaders have to focus on engaging people or teams of people, balancing competing priorities, defining and communicating direction in a way that inspires and compels, and using the resources on hand to their full potential.

The leader isn't always the one out front waving the flag, with the band marching behind her. Leadership isn't about who gets credit for the work, or doing the work one's self, or looking good to customers or other stakeholders. True leadership is about *gaining willing cooperation about where to go and how to get there, and then using patience and skill to motivate and guide everyone there.*

Leadership can be designated ("congratulations, you've been promoted!"), or can emerge naturally from within a group ("we value that you've got such great experience and/or insights"). It can be situationally dependent ("you're the only one with experience with this new system"), or can be role-related ("you're leading the team as part of your job"). But in every case, the leader has to be on his or her toes to handle the variability of change. People are different and are not consistent, resources come and go, and the amount of information we have at any given time is in flux.

The day that Luis Urzua went to work before the collapse, he had no idea how quickly everything would change. Fortunately, he had a core set of leadership skills, values, and principles that let him respond quickly to an emergency. And he was willing to step up and take on the burden of leadership (in this case knowing that the group depended upon his leadership for their very survival) when he could have broken down and waited for someone else to do something.

At Dale Carnegie Training we've seen leaders from all walks of life demonstrate incredible leadership skills like these in all kinds of situations. Never has it been more evident than during the recent pandemic. Leaders had to flex with ongoing uncertainty, while juggling the demands of protecting people and the bottom line. In many cases, we had to learn how to manage a remote team of people who had no idea how to work remotely. Leadership is enough of a challenge without the methods of interacting changing practically overnight.

Why put in the hard work? Because leaders impact the lives of their followers, as well as the whole culture in which they operate. From small "mom and pop" businesses to global corporations, the relationship that the leader has with his or her people makes the difference between success and failure in a company.

What is Leadership?

At Dale Carnegie Training, we believe that leadership is about working through and with others in trusting and dynamic relationships that inspire, engage, and align efforts to realize desired organizational outcomes. Great leaders capture the energy and talent from those they lead and accomplish results far greater than a less dynamic leader would.

This can differ from "management." As we define it, "leadership" is about the people side of getting things done, and "management" is the process side. Every organization needs both leadership and management. Both elements are necessary, yet not individually sufficient.

In our experience studying the most successful leaders from almost every country on Earth, we've discovered five common qualities that differentiate excellent leaders from others.

Outstanding leaders:

1. **Take responsibility for the future**
2. **Build a culture of trust**
3. **Create a culture for collaboration**
4. **Communicate effectively**
5. **Demonstrate reliability**

Every one of these qualities matters for the success of the leader, their team, and the organization. That's what *LEAD!* is about. We'll delve into the elements that form these five qualities and how those qualities translate into results. We'll uncover the personal elements that make a leader effective, and how the leader can then use the power of influence to bring out the best in others. We'll look at how the culture of the organization can affect the kinds of results that allow it to become a leader in its industry.

At its core, though, leadership is a human endeavor. Leaders model the timeless Human Relations Principles that Dale Carnegie taught us that lead to connection, cooperation, and collaboration. In order to succeed as a leader, one must blend performance needs with human needs. This is true whether we're responsible for an accounting team or trying to keep a group of miners alive while trapped underground.

In this book we look at how to balance the needs of the emerging leader to maximize employee performance with their needs as people. But, it's more than knowing and understanding the people side of leadership—it's actively and intentionally seeking opportunities to apply this knowledge and empower those around us, since it's all about them. This book will both inform and throw down a challenge to find ways to apply what you've learned so that you can create an engaged, loyal, passionate, and productive team.

Anyone Can Become a Leader

Dale Carnegie Training offers leadership training in almost every country in the world, and has for decades. This book is a reflection of what we've learned across cultures, industries, demographics, and hierarchies. We've worked to boil down the challenge of leadership for whatever challenge we're facing.

The following graphic illustrates the Dale Carnegie Model of Leadership Success, and is the framework for our book.

Dale Carnegie Model of Leadership Success

The ideas flow from individual attributes to behavioral applications that lead to outcomes and results. The foundation of leadership is the ability to actively and intentionally role model what good leadership is for others. This may require of us a mindset shift. The application of tools and processes come afterward.

But it's not enough to role model leadership behavior when we remember. We're actually being a role model all the time. People are watching us and either want to be like us, or want to be different from us. To be an effective leader, we have to live our lives as a *positive* role model. It's about having Trust, Empathy, and getting Willing Cooperation.

This means being self-aware, accountable, others-focused, and strategic. The chapters in Part One delve more deeply into just how a leader can become a positive role model, and it all starts with self-reflection.

30 Dale Carnegie's Human Relations Principles

At the core of everything we do at Dale Carnegie Training is the foundation of the Human Relations Principles that Dale Carnegie created many years ago. It amazes us how relevant these ideas are to modern life. In fact, if we are faced with a challenge, all we need to do is to look at these principles and see how it can improve the situation. Here are the classic principles that truly have stood the test of time.

Build Trust
BE A FRIENDLIER PERSON
1. Don't criticize, condemn, or complain.
2. Give honest, sincere appreciation.
3. Arouse in the other person an eager want.
4. Become genuinely interested in other people.
5. Smile.
6. Remember that a person's name is to that person the sweetest and most important sound in any language.
7. Be a good listener. Encourage others to talk about themselves.
8. Talk in terms of the other person's interests.
9. Make the other person feel important—and do it sincerely.

Gain Cooperation
WIN PEOPLE TO YOUR WAY OF THINKING
10. The only way to get the best of an argument is to avoid it.
11. Show respect for the other person's opinions—never say, "you're wrong."
12. If you are wrong, admit it quickly and emphatically.
13. Begin in friendly way.
14. Get the other person saying "yes, yes" immediately.
15. Let the other person do a great deal of the talking.
16. Let the other person feel the idea is his or hers.
17. Try honestly to see things from the other person's point of view.
18. Be sympathetic with the other person's ideas and desires.

19. Appeal to the nobler motives.
20. Dramatize your ideas.
21. Throw down a challenge.

Lead Change
BE A LEADER
22. Begin with praise and honest appreciation.
23. Call attention to people's mistakes indirectly.
24. Talk about your own mistakes before criticizing the other person.
25. Ask questions, instead of giving direct orders.
26. Let the other person save face.
27. Praise the slightest improvements and praise every improvement. "Be hearty in your approbation and lavish in your praise."
28. Give the other person a fine reputation to live up to.
29. Use encouragement. Make the fault seem easy to correct.
30. Make the other person happy about doing the thing you suggest.

Part One

*Unleashing Leadership In Yourself:
Improving Your Inner Leader*

Part One: Unleashing Leadership In Yourself will cover the first part of the Dale Carnegie Model of Leadership Success—Role Modeling the behaviors we want to see in others.

Dale Carnegie Model of Leadership Success

Role Model	Apply	Outcomes	Results: *Your* Desired Performance Results
Self-Aware			
Accountability	Human Relations Principles	Trust & Personal Growth	
		Positive Change & Organizational Growth	
Others-Focused		Engagement & Agility	
Strategic	Appropriate Tools & Processes	Common Direction & Innovation	

Within this framework, we'll integrate Dale Carnegie's first Human Relations Principles

1. Don't criticize, condemn, or complain.
2. Give honest, sincere appreciation.
3. Arouse in the other person an eager want.
4. Become genuinely interested in other people.
5. Smile.
6. Remember that a person's name is to that person the sweetest and most important sound in any language.
7. Be a good listener. Encourage others to talk about themselves.
8. Talk in terms of the other person's interests.
9. Make the other person feel important—and do it sincerely.

Together, these ideas will create a solid foundation for improving your inner leader.

It's time to stop doing, and start leading

1. SELF-AWARENESS

"Fran, can I talk to you for a minute?" Warren Cantel was standing at the office door of his mentor, Fran Bianco.

Fran Bianco was the Senior Human Resources Director for a national restaurant chain, and Warren was her direct report. A forty-something balding man with a slight paunch and glasses, Warren resembled a kind uncle more than a cut-throat businessman. He'd been an outstanding HR Analyst, and Fran had promoted him to management two months ago but he'd been struggling ever since. As she looked at his worried face, she wondered—not for the first time—if she'd made a mistake in promoting him.

"Sure, Warren, come on in." Fran closed out the window of her computer monitor and gave him her full attention. "What can I do for you?"

Sighing, Warren sat down. "It's Carl. I keep asking him to create the job descriptions for the hiring event next month and he's blowing me off. I'm being as nice as I can . . . I know he's having some personal issues at home so I'm giving him leeway, but really. This is getting ridiculous. He promises to get them to me and then just doesn't do it. I just feel like he doesn't respect me at all and I'm at my wits end."

"What have you tried?" Fran asked.

"Well, first, we had a meeting and I explained what I needed and when. I thought the meeting went well, but then the agreed upon deadline came and . . . nothing. He just ignored it. When I asked him where they were, he gave me some excuse and said he'd have them in a few days. A few days later it was some other excuse. I sent him text messages and e-mails to remind him but he never even responded. Instead, he took three days of personal leave. Should I just do it myself and deal with him later? It would only take me about an hour and then they would be done."

Fran had seen this before in new managers that had been promoted from within a group. Oftentimes, former peers had trouble seeing the new manager as a leader, largely because the manager had trouble shifting their own identity from the person who "does something" to a person who "gets something done through and with others."

"I don't think you should be the one to do it Warren. I'd like you to try something else first." Fran understood that in order for Warren to get his direct

reports to respect him as their leader, he needed to shift his own self-perception first. "I think we need to work on helping you see yourself as a leader, first."

"Okay, Fran. I trust you." *Warren ran a hand over his balding pate.* "I'll do just about anything at this point because it's not only Carl. It's the whole team. Tell me what to do."

In order for us to get people to follow our leadership, we've got to see ourselves as their role model. We can't just tell people what to do and hope it gets done—or worse yet, do it ourselves. Instead, we must embrace the very qualities we want to grow in our direct reports. This involves delving into concepts of Self-Awareness, Accountability, Others-Focus, and Strategic thinking.

> *The transition to leadership first happens in the mind.*

Pallavi Jha, Chairperson and Managing Director of Dale Carnegie Training India, shares the following wisdom for the emerging leader. "The transition to leadership happens in the mind. For someone who is a first time leader cutting his or her teeth, the transition has to happen in the mind. No underachiever becomes a leader. Assuming you are already confident and assertive, the biggest challenge is that you have to stop doing what you did to get there. The skills that got you promoted are not the same skills that will make you an effective leader. Managers end up managing their own peers. It's a relationship challenge. You were like me and now you're my boss."

As in our story with Warren Cantel, the first step in becoming an effective leader is to shift our perspective from "doer" to "leader." And that comes from self-awareness.

Cynthia Miller* was in tears. She'd just received the results of her 360-degree feedback evaluation, and she was shocked at the results. A senior-level manager at a pharmaceutical company, Cynthia managed the accounting division and reported directly to the CFO. A very logical, "left-brained" person, she had a deep understanding of the processes and procedures of accounting and believed that if her direct reports just applied those methods consistently, they would achieve the same results.

When Cynthia had been asked to assess her own leadership, she felt she was doing a pretty good job of running meetings, carefully explaining the right way for things to be done, and bringing up any issues to be handled as a group.

"I thought they liked me!" she said to the consultant who was going through the results with her. But the "confidential" comments section in the back contained brutally honest feedback that was hard to ignore. Respondents said things like, "She is a hardass who only wants things done her way," and "She delegates but then doesn't give us the resources we need and then panics and takes the project back, complaining that she has to do everything herself."

---

* Names have been changed for privacy.

"If you mess up at work, you can be sure she'll bring it up in a meeting."

How could it be that Cynthia was so out of sync with her perceptions of her leadership and those of her direct reports?

Now consider the example of Mark Pilsner. Like Cynthia, he is a senior-level leader, but instead of pharmaceuticals, his company is a large healthcare organization. Mark is the liaison between the organization and the many external agencies it works with to conduct research. Every day finds Mark giving presentations, being interviewed, and representing the company in the public eye.

When it comes to leading his division, though, Mark considers himself a "straight shooter" who is honest and open with his direct reports and expects the same from them. He'll give praise when it's warranted, but he has no desire to applaud when people don't live up to their own performance standards. He knows this makes him unpopular, but he figures that's the price he has to pay to get high performance from his people. His 360-degree performance evaluation was no surprise to him. His people called him "arrogant," a "know it all," and worst of all, "disrespectful."

How does this happen? In both cases, Cynthia and Mark are ineffective leaders with department cultures that hurt performance as well as morale. In one case, the feedback blindsides the leader because she thinks that the way she is leading is the right way to lead. In the other case, the leader knows he's not popular, but still believes that he's effective.

All of us, whether we are in a leadership role or not, have blind spots. These are aspects of ourselves that we're unaware of. Sometimes other people can see them and we can't, and other times these are areas of growth that are yet to be revealed to anyone.

Blind Spots Versus Self-Awareness

Since we all have blind spots, illuminating them can help us see areas of both strength and opportunity for growth. Elizabeth Haberberger, President of Dale Carnegie Training of St. Louis shares a story that illustrates how discovering our blind spots as a leader can make a transformative difference.

> "A few years ago, the CEO of a $4 billion construction company hired a project manager. We'll call him Scott, to protect his privacy. About a year later, Scott's younger brother Kevin (also not his real name) was hired on as well. For the next year the two brothers worked as peers, but in the second year Kevin was promoted over Scott. Scott went to the CEO and asked, 'Why did you promote my brother? I've been here longer and I was next in line for promotion.' The CEO sat Scott down and said, 'I didn't promote you because, frankly, no one likes you. No one trusts you. You're good at your job, but being good at your job isn't enough. You don't have the relationships with your team that Kevin does.' Scott was angry and stormed out. It can be hard to shine a light on someone's blind spot, and the CEO had the courage to do it.

"The next day Scott came back into the CEO's office and said, 'You're right. I think I kind of knew it all along. But, I don't want to be that person. I don't want to be the one that no one likes or trusts. Tell me what I need to do.' The CEO sent Scott to leadership training where he became curious, was willing to change, and tried new skills and approaches. He learned how to develop connections with people, gain their cooperation, and create collaboration. Now Scott is a senior leader in their organization."

This story beautifully illustrates the fact that we need both self-awareness and the knowledge of what to do differently and the desire for change.

What are the conditions that led Cynthia to be so blind about her weaknesses? Now that she is aware, does she know what to do to change it?

With Mark, he is unwilling to change. Even if he's given the tools and knowledge that would help him lead differently, he's not likely to do it because he doesn't believe he needs to change.

The losers in both cases are their followers. Cynthia and Mark's leadership don't inspire others to greater levels of productivity. Instead they inspire anger, resentment, and a feeling of dread coming to work.

The organizations suffer too, because if the culture allows one leader to lead this way, it can spread like wildfire. This can cause people to leave, which is time consuming and expensive for the organization.

Cynthia and Mark lose out too. Because even if they are not consciously aware of the problems, like Cynthia, or are aware of them but disregard them, like Mark, it's virtually impossible to be unaffected by a toxic work environment. This can significantly decrease the likelihood they will be promoted.

Is it a matter, then, of giving these leaders more technology, more resources, or more funding? No. It's about giving them self-awareness and the tools to role model positive behaviors for the people they lead.

Reputation versus Identity

What's the difference between reputation and identity? Reputation is how others see us and identity is how we see ourselves. In the case above, Cynthia and Mark each had the identity of a strong leader, but the reputation as a poor one. In our example with Warren Cantel, he knows he's not being an effective leader, and his direct reports would agree. What these examples are illustrating are the difference between one's identity and reputation. We have to have the self-awareness to accurately assess our leadership ability and to then focus on building a reputation as a role model.

The greater the gap between our identity and our reputation, the less effective we will be at leading.

How can a leader make sure that his or her identity and reputation are aligned? The first step is self-awareness.

The Qualities That Determine Self-Awareness

What, then, are the qualities of a person who is self-aware?
- Self-directed
- Self-regulated
- Develops self
- Confident

Let's look a little more closely at each of these.

Being *self-directed* means having an inner sense of guidance. It's about wanting to achieve goals and then taking the actions needed to achieve them. We all have goals we want to achieve, and the difference between a pipe dream and a goal is whether we actually take the steps to make it happen. Comedian Steve Harvey tells the story of standing up in elementary school and in a soft, stuttering voice, announced that he was going to be on television. His classmates and teacher all laughed at him. Harvey says that he sends a brand new television set to that teacher every year to remind her that he achieved his goal through his deliberate hard work.

Being *self-regulated* means having the maturity to control our own behavior. It's about setting up a structure, whether it be a budget, a time management plan, or some other system to guide our behavior to achieve our goals, and then following it. Alan Mulally was the CEO of Ford starting in 2006 and led the company from a $12 billion loss to profitability in three years in the midst of the Great Recession. In his "People First" culture, he advocated that everyone should know the plan, the status against the plan, and the areas that need special attention. If people didn't want to work this way, his response was a calm, "that's okay." And he gently suggested that they look for another opportunity. He didn't get angry because he cared about the people as individuals, and recognized that the culture he created wasn't for every leader, and was a shift from the way the company had traditionally worked.

Develops self is about continued growth. It's about reading books and taking classes, learning new things and improving existing skills. Indra Nooyi is a passionate champion for asking questions, being curious, and always seeking to learn more. The Former Pepsico CEO tells us never to settle for the knowledge we have, but to go further.

Finally, being *confident* isn't only about being extroverted and having charisma. It's about having an inner knowing that we can effect change in ourselves and others. When the mine collapsed on Luis Urzua in Chile, he didn't spend much time wondering if he had the proper qualifications to lead a group of miners to keep them alive, he got into action with a self-confidence that this is what was needed for the moment.

Don't Underestimate Yourself

Author Leo Tolstoy once said, "It's not who we are that holds us back it's who we think we're not." Gaweed El

Nakeeb, Carnegie Master Trainer in Egypt advises emerging leaders, "Don't underestimate yourself. Push out of your comfort zone. Too often we waste life thinking we don't have means or resources. Just try. Don't hold yourself back. Go for it."

He goes on to say, "Knowing how to be a good leader is really easy. There is a ton of information available. It's not a lack of knowledge. It's about having the right attitude and the discipline to apply what you need to apply. It's suppressing your own ego and saying, 'I need to learn something new and be open to learning something new.'"

Become a Leader of Influence

Leaders of influence work to draw out the experience of the members of a group to accomplish a task, and let others step in to provide the expertise, themselves stepping back to lead from behind and let them own the task, so that in the end the team says, "we did this," rather than pointing at the leader and saying, "she did this." In *Good to Great*, author Jim Collins provides many examples of CEOs of companies that were successful for decades that most of us have never heard of. They were focused on building companies and teams that would be successful, rather than having to be "The Leader" who made it happen.

But then there are the *leaders of power* who need to be right, who need to show that they are the ones with the expertise. They lead with ego, diminishing everyone around them. There are many, many famous leaders who focus on burnishing their reputations so that they appear on the covers of magazines and newspapers as "The Leader" who made it happen. While they may be successful in the short term, in most cases they don't build leaders and talent around them, they become the critical source of success that is not sustainable.

A leader can have the most talented, intelligent team, but if he or she is plagued with ineffective leadership skills and thinking, he or she will not gain the Trust, Empathy, or Willing Cooperation of the team. It doesn't matter that we have a great team if we're not able to lead them to success. Self-Awareness is the first step to this outcome.

Self-Awareness Versus Selfishness

There is a difference between self-awareness and being selfish. Self-awareness causes us to see the connection between past experiences and current behavior. When we know our values and our emotional triggers, have a clear idea of our worldview and know our personality, we are better able to see ourselves in others. When we are selfish, we constantly shine the spotlight on ourselves, when in fact leadership is not about the leader, it's about how the leader serves the people they lead.

It takes a leader who values personal growth to focus on self-awareness because they'll see the connection between personal growth and increasingly effective leadership. The more the leader grows, the more the leader can focus on others to help them grow, develop, and bring out their greatness.

Are You Self-Aware?

Ironically, most people think they are more self-aware than they really are. Higher level leaders in particular overvalue their skills as compared to other people's perceptions.

Why is this? First, the higher we go in an organization, the less likely we are to find people willing to provide candid feedback. People will often "kiss the butt" of their boss in order to look good themselves. This leads to a distorted view of reality.

Also, sometimes one's willingness to listen shrinks. The tendency is to attribute one's success to one's own skills and talents, and so by definition the one who is higher in the organizational structure must know more and be more skilled than his or her subordinates—at least in the minds of some leaders.

How To Develop Self-Awareness

To be a self-aware leader, the first place we need to look is in the mirror. We should take every opportunity to conduct self-assessments. We also need to gather the opinions of others—and not just from people who will say nice things. Get feedback from people with whom we have conflict. Take trainings and read books. Reflect each day on our interactions with others and how we impacted them. Develop a "self-awareness routine" by which we start each day with an intent for how we want to be, and then reflect on whether we achieved that intent. Dale Carnegie team leader Jonathan Vehar tells of an associate who took the opportunity to have twenty conversations with family, co-workers, friends, and clients to get input on how they showed up. They were looking to understand the kind of role model they were. These conversations focused on understanding strengths and weaknesses. "Pat" reported that he was looking for "the dirt," the really unpleasant things that he could fix. He found some important areas, but also heard some strengths that he'd never realized before. These strengths became the foundation for future success.

Identify Blind Spots

As we mentioned earlier, blind spots can be the death of effective leadership. Dale Carnegie Training's research identified four core areas where we can be unaware of our impact. These are things that we may think we are doing well, but in reality are not.

1. Praise and appreciation. Most people say they don't get enough feedback and especially praise and appreciation. And most of us realize we don't give nearly enough.
2. Admit when we are wrong. Sometimes we focus too much on why we did it, or covering it up, when really what's needed is for us to emphatically admit that we goofed and then work on correcting it.
3. Listen, respect, and value employee opinions. By virtue of where we sit, leaders don't and can't know

what's happening on the front line, which is why we need to actively seek it out and believe it, rather than discount it because it may be different than what we believe.
4. Employees can trust them to be honest with themselves and others. While there are times that leaders can't share information, the more transparent and honest we are, the more trust and loyalty we build in our teams.

Having an awareness of these blind spots may help all of us better see the gap between our actual behavior and our desired behavior, when getting the best from those who look to us for leadership. Leaders who work to identify blind spots in these four areas and learn to overcome them on a personal level have considerable potential to impact the employee experience of those who report to them and interact with them.

When it comes to evaluating the impact of our own behavior, keep these tips in mind:
- Assume that we are not objective when assessing our own capabilities. That means we need help. There are a variety of 360-degree feedback tools available that can provide insight into the perceptions of those with whom you work.
- Prepare yourself for feedback. It can be difficult to set egos aside, and many people benefit from learning adaptive techniques that help them approach and accept feedback constructively.

- Appreciate the intent. While getting feedback that reveals blind spots can be uncomfortable, remember that it's also difficult to give constructive feedback. Chances are, those providing it are trying to help.
- Disrupt routines. We are blind to the things around us when we become set in our own ways and fall into routines regarding how we engage others, including reacting to issues, running meetings or coaching our employees.
- Just do it. Given the importance of these leadership behaviors, there's no downside to simply taking action to become even better at them. The simple act of learning can also encourage greater self-insight, which means there's twofold benefit to taking action: becoming aware of and simultaneously working to improve one's performance of these crucial behaviors for motivating employees.

We can never completely eliminate our blind spots; they are part of human nature. But through candid self-reflection combined with focused effort, we can safely steer ourselves toward becoming the exceptional leaders we want to be.

With self-awareness, adopt what is known as a "learner's mind." Be open and curious, be okay with making mistakes and being wrong. Even if we strive to have impeccably high standards, we must leave our ego at the door.

In the next chapter, we'll cover another important element of leadership—accountability.

Key Takeaways

- At its core, leadership is a way to achieve results through and with other people.
- "Leadership" is about the people side of getting things done, and "management" is the process side.
- Outstanding leaders:
    1. Take responsibility for the future
    2. Build a culture of trust
    3. Create a culture for collaboration
    4. Communicate effectively
    5. Demonstrate reliability
- In order to get people to follow our leadership, we must embrace the very qualities we want to grow in our direct reports. This involves delving into concepts of Self-Awareness, Accountability, Others-Focus, and Strategic thinking.
- The transition to leadership happens in the mind.
- Blind Spots are aspects of ourselves that we can't see. Sometimes others can see them, and sometimes no one can see them.
- When others can see a blind spot and we can't, there is a difference between identity and reputation.
- The greater the gap between identity and reputation, the less effective the leadership.
- The key to closing the gap is increased self-awareness.
- Self-awareness can grow when we are open to receiving feedback from a variety of sources.

2. ACCOUNTABILITY

The envelope had been sitting on his desk for three days now, and Warren Cantel knew he was going to have to open it eventually. His boss, Fran, had orchestrated a 360-degree feedback evaluation for him, and the results were in. Warren had filled out the lengthy questionnaire, as had Fran and Warren's new peers, and his direct reports (most of whom used to be his peers). He had an appointment with Fran to go over the results tomorrow afternoon, and wanted to be prepared for what his colleagues had said about his leadership ability.

Grabbing the envelope and tearing it open, Warren muttered, "Well, there's no time like the present." As his eyes scanned the first page summary of the results, his heart sank. It was just as he thought. Everyone hated him.

"Warren, they do not hate you." Fran flipped through the results of the survey. "Sure, there are some areas for improvement. There always are. But there is a lot of good here, too. Let me show you."

Over the next hour, Fran showed Warren that the results were not nearly as bad as he'd thought. His bosses (Fran and her boss) rated Warren a four out of five stars in all of the key areas of leadership. His peers were a little lower, at 3.5, largely because they didn't know him all that well. And there was one direct report who dragged down the average with all one star ratings, but the rest of his team gave ratings that skewed positive. Even though the results were supposed to be anonymous, Warren was sure that the low scoring direct report was Carl. Who else could it be?

"It's not important who gave you which ratings, Warren." Fran smiled a little, as if she'd been reading his mind. "What matters is that you are accountable to the team for what they've said. Let's identify three areas for growth that you can share with your direct reports as things you'll work on."

Together, Warren and Fran identified that Warren would work on his listening skills, effective goal setting, and managing progress towards goals. He was relieved that there were no issues with his integrity.

"Thanks a lot, Fran." Warren closed the report and stood to head back to his own office. "I do feel a lot better about things. I'll follow up with everyone and thank them for participating and tell them the three takeaways from the report."

As he walked down the hall to his own office, one thing did still concern him. Carl. How could he improve his relationship with a direct report who was so angry with him?

Accountability is Personal

When we hear the word "accountability," we often think of holding others "accountable" for their actions, their results, or some behaviorally observable action. When we send a team of people off for sales training, we hold them accountable by ensuring that there is an improvement in sales.

While there is a very needed public component to the idea of accountability, it really starts inside. Holding ourselves accountable for the things we say and do are core components of being a positive role model. It's not only about having an image of corporate accountability, but is about what we do and say every day. Our integrity is all about whether we walk our talk.

What do you do when you're in a restaurant and the server leaves an item off your bill? Do you happily pay the lower bill, figuring you got a "discount?" Or do you tell the server of his or her error and pay for what you ordered?

Do you focus on improving your skills and abilities, so that you can make fewer mistakes at work? In order to be an effective role model, we have to be continually improving and growing. It's not enough to rest on our laurels once we've achieved that promotion we feel we earned.

Do you set goals and then make visible progress toward them? Or are you one of those people who are always talking about how "one of these days" they will achieve a personal or professional goal?

How is the quality of your decision making? Do you look at how you make decisions and proactively find ways to make better ones? Or do you keep moving forward without doing the work of self-reflection?

Being accountable on a large scale has to do with being the kind of person who accepts responsibility for the small things.

Anita Zinsmeister, President of Dale Carnegie of Central and Southern New Jersey shares this story.

> "An Executive Vice President at a large pharmaceutical company, doing research and development in clinical pharmacology, was part of a big merger where her company had acquired another team. There was a lot of uncertainty with the merger and the work was critically important. These were specialists with highly technical expertise whose people skills were not as finely developed. Add in many cultural differences and you can imagine the challenges in people working well together. The senior leader wanted to provide some relationship training to facilitate bonding in the team. She realized that she needed to work with the different parts of the business to be successful in influencing change. Ultimately, she was accountable for the outcome here.
>
> "The EVP did a needs assessment and then obtained buy-in to design the training. But instead of just sending the teams in for training to 'get fixed and

come back,' she took the training along with them. And she didn't just sit in the training. She threw herself into it. She took more notes than anyone, gave recognition to others, praised them, and accepted their feedback. As she went through the experience and modeled her desire to lead a successful team that worked well together, the team saw her commitment to them and became increasingly loyal to her leadership. They transformed into a high performing team. It was her level of personal accountability to their success that influenced them. She realized that the timing was critical and that the way to facilitate the group's change was not to *tell* the group how to be. She knew that she needed to role model the actions and attitudes she wanted them to adopt. It worked. The group was eventually singled out in the organization as a high performing team."

No matter how senior your level, keep growing your skills and role model what you want your team to improve

---

The Qualities of Accountability

What, then, are the qualities of someone who is accountable?
- Competent
- Demonstrates honesty and integrity

- Manages progress towards goals
- Makes effective decisions

Let's look a little more closely at each of these.

Someone who is *competent* is someone who is capable of doing the job. This means that when someone gives us a task to do, we can do it. And if we can't, then we quickly gain the skills or get help. The EVP that Anita described realized that as good as she was with people skills, she needed to get better along with the group, even though she and the team members had the technical skills. They needed more to get their jobs done.

Honesty and integrity are very important parts of being accountable. How? Because everyone makes mistakes, and someone who is honest and has integrity will admit to them and work to make it right. This is one of the core tenets of being a powerful role model. Many companies have failed because people didn't own up to their mistakes and spent more time covering them up than fixing them. Volkswagen knew they had a problem with the levels of emissions from their diesel cars for years and didn't fix the problem. As of June of 2020, the scandal had cost the company $33.3 billion and ruined the careers of many people involved.

Manages progress toward goals is another important element of accountability. Goal accomplishment is never linear. Often it's "two steps forward and one step back." Being able to manage this process and continue to make progress toward goals instead of giving up is something that effective leaders role model. In 1942 Chester Carlson patented "xerography," the process behind copy machines, laser and LED printers. The company that introduced the technology, Haloid/Xerox, worked for decades to create a workable machine that was finally introduced in 1960. At various points in the process everyone on the project wanted to give up. Fortunately, there was always a leader there to encourage the team to keep at it until they eventually succeeded and changed how we work to this day.

Makes effective decisions. Note that this does not say "makes perfect decisions all of the time." We can only make decisions based on the information we have at the time, and we're influenced by a lot of external factors. Being accountable means that we make effective decisions as often as possible, and then change them as circumstances warrant. When the COVID-19 crisis first hit in early 2020, Herb Escher, the President of Dale Carnegie of Western New York pulled his team together and told them that no one was going to be laid off and that they were going to shift how they serve their clients now that normal operations of the training company were shut down due to state regulations. With Herb leading the team, and based on input from a loyal client base, they made the decisions to rapidly shift from a face-to-face operation to one that served clients in the virtual space, and within weeks were generating the revenue needed to pay salaries and keep the operation afloat.

Competence

What does it mean to be a "competent" leader? Does it mean that you're the one who is the best subject matter expert? Not necessarily. Is it just a matter of not being an arrogant jerk? No, it's more than that. It's about really embracing our self-identity as a leader. As we've said, the skills and attributes that get us the leadership position are not the ones that necessarily make for a competent leader.

Elizabeth Haberberger puts it this way. "No one knows what they are doing. I come at this from a unique angle. I'm thirty-one and just bought my operation last year and have been figuring it out. Leaders seem like they know what they are doing. Being young and female you get intimidated by leaders with more power and experience but, at first, no one knows what they are doing."

In most cases, there are no prescribed algorithms for the tough decisions that leaders have to make. The reality of leadership is that it's a dance between improvising how to get things done based on experience, evolving information, and a constantly changing environment. There is no book that tells you what your organization needs to do in this situation to get the results you need.

So how do you develop leadership competence? Spend time learning and invest in yourself. Read as much as you can. Warren Buffett, one of the most successful investors in the world, reads five to six hours *per day*. It's one of the things to which he attributes his success, and he encourages his people to do the same. What should we read? There are an infinite number of books. Read, listen to podcasts and other leaders, sit down for networking coffees, peer groups, and speak up. Make time to learn, and then don't be afraid to give your thoughts and opinions even if you don't think you know what you're talking about. If your ideas never get out there no one can see you as a leader.

Elizabeth shared this story. "A year ago we hired someone. We have a small team and Jackie was the sixth. Everyone else had been there since before me. Jackie is a rock star. She had turned fifty, and was really successful, with thirty years of experience. I started feeling really insecure. She was going to report to me? Did she think I'm an idiot? I worried that she would wonder, 'Why did I leave this corporate job to work for you?' But, we practiced what we preach in terms of leadership and we did one-on-one conversations and talked about her personal and professional life. We actually did what we teach in our classes. Every week we asked, 'What do you need more of or less of?' We related everything to the core values, vision, mission, three year plan and checked in on how it all worked out this week. When we're feeling insecure as a leader, we need to let our actions be our guide. As a leader we do those little things on a daily and weekly basis. We can't always see the changes in ourselves—we don't know. We have to trust that the small actions that we take over time compound and create a strong leader."

A Culture of Integrity

How We Do One Thing is How We Do Everything

Ryan Turner runs a popular Huntington Beach breakfast spot called The Sugar Shack that his family has had since the 1960s. One morning, a couple came in and happily ordered breakfast in the world-famous surfer's diner. The man was about 90% finished with his oversized bowl of oatmeal when he saw a stray hair in the bowl. The man and his dining companion were both blonde, and the hair was not.

The man called the waiter over, who spoke with Ryan. As would be expected, the management apologized profusely. Most restaurant managers would take the oatmeal off the bill, and Ryan was not an exception. But Ryan Turner took it another step. He gave both diners their breakfast for free.

He understood that owning up to the mistake and going above and beyond to make it right was worth far more than a $40 tab. Ryan truly got the concept that "how we do one thing is how we do everything." And that attitude has filtered through to his entire staff, and has become part of the culture of the restaurant. One of Dale Carnegie's principles is "If you are wrong, admit it quickly and emphatically."

Although this part of LEAD! is focused on the individual qualities of leaders, the truth is that we really can't separate out the integrity of a leader from the rest of the company.

If a company has a culture of "looking the other way," or "It's not our problem," they are likely to choose a leader who shares those values. This is one of the reasons the CEO of Volkswagen was fired as a result of the diesel emissions scandal. Of course, that's not going to be part of any job description, but what tends to happen is that a leader with integrity who comes into an organization with a culture of "looking the other way" is going to experience huge challenges. The change has to come at the cultural level.

How does this happen? If we are a leader who espouses values of honesty and integrity, but we're operating in an environment that doesn't necessarily share those values, what can we do?

Moral Courage

The answer, of course, is what we are talking about in this book. Effective leadership. It can be hard to turn around the culture of an entire company or even our team. But the leader sets the tone, and has a significant impact on the culture. Either way, it requires clearly stating the values by which employees need to operate.

In May of 2018, Starbucks CEO Kevin Johnson ordered all of its US stores to close for the day so that the nearly 175,000 employees could receive racial bias training after an incident where two black customers were arrested after asking to use the bathroom.

"I've spent the last few days in Philadelphia with my leadership team listening to the community, learning what we did wrong, and the steps we need to take to fix it," said Starbucks CEO Kevin Johnson. "While this is not limited to Starbucks, we're committed to being a part of the solution. Closing our stores for racial bias training is just one step in a journey that requires dedication from every level of our company and partnerships in our local communities*."

Some may argue that a one-day training isn't enough and that it was more for PR than actual cultural change.

---

* https://stories.starbucks.com/press/2018/starbucks-to-close-stores-nationwide-for-racial-bias-education-may-29/

But no one can claim that Kevin Johnson didn't explicitly state the values he expected his team members to exemplify.

How can we tell whether or not a leader has integrity? It's not based on what we say. And it's not merely something we can observe based on the behaviors they engage in.

The fact is, we can never know what goes on inside someone's mind. But, when a leader demonstrates that he or she is behaving according to a set of explicitly stated values, especially under adverse conditions, followers see the leader as having integrity and courage. Integrity is about "walking the talk and talking the walk."

Honesty and Integrity

Kelly Thomas had been saving for her daughter's high school graduation trip for more than a year. Unlike a lot of teenage girls, Caylee wanted to take a road trip to Los Angeles with her mother to audition for *America's Got Talent*.

Kelly spent weeks researching every aspect of the trip. From booking a house through Airbnb near the audition venue in Pasadena to renting a fun convertible for the drive from New Mexico, it was going to be a mother-daughter adventure that would make memories to last a lifetime.

Everything went well for the first leg of the trip, as Kelly and Caylee drove from Albuquerque to Phoenix. The first Airbnb they stayed in was fine, and they headed out to make the rest of the trip to the greater Los Angeles area. They cheered as they approached Pasadena and saw where Caylee would be auditioning. LA seemed really large and intimidating though, and they were looking forward to the modest bungalow they'd booked.

About an hour before they were to check in, they received a message through the Airbnb app that there was a plumbing problem with the bungalow, and the owner felt terribly and would upgrade to a larger unit nearby.

Kelly wasn't sure, as she hadn't had time to research the new neighborhood, but was feeling pressured because they were already in Pasadena with all of their belongings and had nowhere to sleep that night. She'd already paid the fee for the room, so she just agreed to the change through the Airbnb app.

Things went from bad to worse as they arrived at the new room. It was in a terrible neighborhood and was nothing more than a sparsely decorated room with furniture that looked like it had been dragged in from the trash. Caylee was in tears, and when Kelly tried to contact the owner, he was unresponsive.

She then took it to the Airbnb customer service system, but was told that since she'd agreed to the change, there was little they could do. She could open a ticket and after review might be able to get a partial refund. But, the agent told her, she should have cancelled the reservation instead of agreeing to the change.

When Kelly went to contact the owners of the unit again, they had deactivated their listings. Kelly had been scammed and the Airbnb policies placed blame on her.

In the end, Kelly was able to get a partial refund, but the whole experience left a mark on what should have been a perfect vacation.

This story might seem like an unfortunate exception, but it's not. Increasingly, there are people in the "gig economy" who are taking advantage of a poorly regulated industry to scam the general public. Whose responsibility is it to prevent these things from happening? The Airbnb website has its rules and policies about cancellations and refunds clearly stated. But, when you're stuck in an unfamiliar city with nowhere to sleep, it can be difficult to know what to do. Although the problem was not directly the fault of Airbnb or its management, do they bear any responsibility to the customer who is scammed by someone using their platform?

The reality of being a leader is that things happen for which we are accountable, and things happen for which we're not accountable but reflect negatively on us, whether or not we knew about it or had any control over the situation. While it's not fair, it's part of the job. How we handle ourselves and react to the situation is where we demonstrate our leadership abilities.

It can be said that the most important function that honesty and integrity can serve in a company is that it prevents the kinds of problems and mistakes that grow into larger issues. No one wants to be the "snitch," who alerts others of wrongdoing. But "looking the other way" can become telling small lies, which can become the sin of omission and not saying something.

The leader has to emphasize honesty over other values, and the way it's done is by being a role model in transparency. It might look bad to have to delay a project or admit a mistake, but it's not nearly as bad as the potential crises that can occur when we just try to cover up our mistake.

Manages progress towards goals

In early 2018, video game retailer GameStop announced a bold new diversification strategy to offset industry changes that were eating away at their profits. Previously, GameStop's greatest source of revenue came from their "pre-owned" segment, and they incentivized customers to sell back used video games and systems.

But in recent years, more and more players began to shift to purchasing digital copies of games and playing collaboratively online. To compensate for this GameStop diversified by adding 1,300 technology brands and began adding marketing to their collectibles business.

But when the CEO of the company became ill and had to step down and a new CEO was promoted from within, his new goal was to fix the operational issues and scale back the diversification while closing hundreds of stores in an attempt to stop the financial bleeding.

It could be said that the scaling back of the company was caused by a technology-driven industry-wide shift. Yet consider the fact that in 2019, virtually every major tech company was hustling to develop a streaming video game platform, and video game companies were at the center of an all-out race to be the first to be able to stream gaming to any device regardless of processing power. Clearly, this is not a dying industry, and it's a very dynamic one with plenty of opportunities for expansion and innovation.

What does that do to the perception of GameStop's ability to achieve goals? How is the image of GameStop's leadership affected by the fact that the company that was once an industry leader is closing stores and being left in the dust? The video rental chain Blockbuster faced a similar situation when consumers made the shift to streaming video. They failed while Netflix thrived. Kodak faced a similar situation when consumers moved to digital photography and abandoned film. Certainly there were plenty of precedents, yet the company was unable to adapt.

Whether it's an international company like GameStop, or an individual manager who consistently fails to meet product launch timelines, making progress and achieving goals—even in a dynamic or turbulent environment—is an important part of accountability. It's like the sports team who loses the championship. Who gets fired? Not the star player. The coach. As the leader, we are accountable for the performance.

How can we, as leaders, manage progress toward goals, on both an individual and group level? By remembering the five parts of GOALS with this useful acronym*.

G: The GET Step Decide what it is you want to get and write it down. Make a list of all the things you'd like to do and be, a list of all the places you want to go, and the things you want to accomplish. Do you want your group to hit a specific sales target? What are the metrics of success that you want your direct reports to achieve? Be as specific as possible with what you want to achieve and write it down.

O: The ORGANIZE Step After you've identified the results you want from your team, organize your plan by listing

---

* http://www.dalecarnegiewaymddc.com/2011/05/09/4-steps-to-easy-goal-setting/

every step that it will take to get you what you want. If you want to increase sales, for example, break it down into steps. List each of your direct reports and their contribution to the goal. Who needs to do what? Be as thorough as possible and break it down into as many steps as it will take.

Then, organize your plan by prioritizing your list. What needs to be done first? Make a list of the order that will best accomplish your goal. If some of the items on your list look overwhelming, break them down into more manageable pieces.

A: The ACTION Step Take some action every day to move you toward your goals. Write down the three or four things that are most important to do every day, week, and month to move you toward your goals and plan when to do them. Meet with your direct reports regularly, both as individuals and as a team to see how things are progressing. Make sure that everyone knows what they need to be doing to move the team toward the goal.

L: The LIST Step Make lists as you go. List what you want. List how to get there. List the steps you need to take to accomplish your actions. List the obstacles that might get in your way. List how to overcome them. List your action steps. By writing things down, you form a commitment to get them done and give your subconscious some work to do! And then follow the lists! Be deliberate about checking the lists at least daily and prioritizing what needs to be done first and getting them done one by one.

S: The SUCCESS Step Enjoy your success! Each time you accomplish part or all of a goal you'll boost your confidence and give you the motivation to go on and finish something else. The feeling of progress is critical to our happiness, and each time we accomplish part of the goal we reinforce our ability to succeed.

Now that we've talked about managing progress toward goals we can move on to the final quality associated with accountability—effective decision making.

Makes effective decisions

How do we know whether or not a decision we've made is an effective one? Is it by the outcome of the decision, or from having a system in place by which we make decisions?

Dale Carnegie Training suggests the following four pronged approach to decision making and problem solving.

First, ask, *"What is the problem?"* While this sounds straightforward, it's not as simple as it seems. The definition of the problem is what shapes the solution. We have to make sure we're solving the right problem.

For example, "We don't have enough customers" sounds like a good statement of a problem. The solution would seem to be "Get more customers."

But, is that really the problem? Not necessarily. A better question might be, "How can we attract a new set of customers?" Exploring why we're not attracting new customers leads to a different answer and set of solutions.

Harley Davidson is a manufacturer of high-end motorcycles. They're famous for their large, heavy road bikes.

But today's younger riders prefer lighter, leaner bikes. They want motorcycles for "ease of transportation" rather than the status that comes with having a Harley.*

If Harley Davidson asked the question, "How can we attract a new set of customers?" What decisions would that question lead to? Harley Davidson is launching an all-electric motorcycle and offering nationwide riding lessons.

If they had just asked the question "How can we get more customers?" without the understanding of *why* people weren't purchasing, they might have invested more marketing dollars to the same old customers, or in advertising their existing products to a generation that isn't interested in buying them. Instead, by identifying the right problem, they are able to make more effective decisions.

Second, ask *"What are the causes of the problem?"* Sometimes, the answer is clear. As in the case of Harley, the cause of the problem was that younger riders want different things in a motorcycle. The industry is changing while their traditional customer base is aging.

But what happens when the cause of our problem is ill defined? A great example of this is what happened to GoPro.**

GoPro literally defined the action camera industry. In fact, after a decade of incredible growth, the company held one of the most successful tech IPOs of 2014, and continued to see massive growth year after year. Until things

---

* https://www.cnbc.com/2019/01/25/actually-young-people-really-could-kill-harley-davidson.html

** https://www.inc.com/magazine/201802/tom-foster/gopro-camera-drone-challenges.html

changed. The company stock that had been worth $98 bottomed out to less than $8 a share.

What was the cause? Was it the development of phone cameras that could take video? Was it an over-investment in too much staff, too many engineers, and too many new products? Could it be the shift in focus from being a "camera company" to a "media company" with its own "Hulu-like" platform?

In truth it was probably all of these. But at the core of these massive corporate decisions was an entrepreneurial leader who wasn't using a systematic process for decision making. It was the classic entrepreneurial "leap and the net will appear" mindset that works great in startups and not so great in large, publicly owned companies. Rather than truly understanding the needs of their customers, they innovated in areas in which their customer wasn't interested, or in creating things that others were already doing.

It boils down to what we have been saying all along. The qualities of the individual leader have dramatic ripple effects outward. By establishing a culture of "damn the torpedoes," GoPro's leaders reinforced that understanding the causes of the problem was less important than taking action.

Third, we suggest asking *"What are the possible solutions?"* Generally, in the beginning of a decision making process, there are only two, maybe three solutions. Invest or don't. Use this vendor or that one. This results in the same old solutions that everyone knows. It's this step that is the second most critical in the process of making effective decisions (behind how we define the challenge).

Inexperienced or ineffective decision makers simply view the existing options as the ones to choose from. Instead of settling for the first couple of options that come to mind, the effective decision maker digs deeper. Asks more questions. Challenges all the assumptions.

Here is an example of questioning assumptions and how it can lead to better decisions. Becky was faced with the difficult task of letting one of her employees go. Her boss, Rick, told her, "The constant fighting between Amy and Pete is making everyone uncomfortable. You need to let one of them go."

Becky tried everything first. She sent them for counseling. She brought in a consultant to get at the root of the problem. Amy told the consultant that they needed to fire Pete, and Pete told the consultant that they needed to fire Amy. The consultant recommended firing them both.

Becky didn't want to do that, but nothing was working. They just kept arguing and sabotaging each other at work. Becky could only see two possible solutions. Fire Amy or fire Pete.

But before she did this, she decided to question her assumptions. Did she really need to fire Amy or Pete? Maybe there was an alternative she hadn't considered. For example, would one of them be willing to transfer to a different location instead?

Becky sat down and talked to each one of them separately. When Becky asked if each person would be willing to relocate, Pete said that his wife and kids were deeply rooted in the community and it wouldn't be possible. But Amy expressed interest. She loved working for the company, but her mother had just fallen ill and she was torn between wanting to stay working for the company and wanting to move closer to her parents.

If Becky had just settled for the first two options on her list, fire Amy or fire Pete, she would have missed an opportunity to keep two valuable employees.

In a very similar situation, Karen Strickholm gave her employees her credit card, told them to go to a nice restaurant and not come back until they had settled their differences otherwise they'd both have to look for another job. Needless to say, they figured it out and made it work for everyone. It wasn't an inexpensive lunch, but it was money well spent, reports Karen.

Bob Galvin, the CEO who led Motorola's tremendous growth from 1959–1986 said, "If you have a hard decision, I respectfully suggest that it is because you have not done sufficient creative thinking... How can you make the best decision if you haven't got the best option? [We've] got to go through the process of being very creative in coming up with that extraordinary option. Then it's easy to select."

Finally, Dale Carnegie Training asks, "What is the best solution?" Notice that this does not say, "What is the perfect solution?" It refers to "given the information we have at the moment, which of the solutions we identified will work the best?" Sometimes we want to avoid a decision because we don't have as much information as we want. Discretion may be warranted, but we will never have all the information we want. In situations where we cannot wait, we have to decide based on what we know.

In the case of Pete and Amy, Becky found that the best solution was to relocate Amy to be closer to her mother. It's possible that the "perfect" solution would have been for Amy and Pete to get along better so that no one needed to leave. That wasn't an option in this case. Finding the best solution is tied to the information that we have at any given time. That's why it's important to ask the right question when looking at what the problem is, and to challenge our assumptions about the cause of the problem. It's that information that leads to the options on the table.

We started this chapter on accountability by saying that accountability is personal. But we've seen numerous instances of how individual leaders and their actions affect the entire organization.

Next, let's look at the next quality of being a role model—being others focused.

Key Takeaways

- Holding ourselves accountable for the things we say and do are core components of being a positive role model
- The qualities of being accountable are:
    1. Competent
    2. Demonstrates honesty and integrity
    3. Manages progress towards goals
    4. Makes effective decisions
- How we do one thing is how we do everything. Being accountable is a way of life.
- Competence in leadership is different than being the best person at the job. It takes a different skillset to be a competent leader. "Stop doing, start leading."
- Integrity and moral courage means living according to an explicit set of values and standing up for those values when we see them being violated.
- To make progress toward goals, use the G.O.A.L.S. Method. Get, Organize, Action, List, Success.
- The four pronged approach to effective decision making is asking "what is the problem." "what are the causes of the problem," "what are the possible solutions," and "what is the best solution?"

3. BEING OTHERS FOCUSED

"I appreciate everyone coming in today," Warren said as he stood at the front of the conference room. "I wanted to share the results of that survey you guys did on me, and let you know what I've decided to work on."

Despite his calm, external appearance, Warren was feeling anxious. He hated public speaking, and this was even worse. He was public speaking about his own weaknesses. Or, "opportunities for growth" as Fran had called them. But to Warren, they felt more like weaknesses that he'd struggled with his whole life.

"So, um, yeah. One of the things that I'm gonna work on is listening skills."

From the back of the room, a voice muttered, "About time..." Warren couldn't be sure but he suspected it came from Carl.

Clearing his throat, he continued. "And goal setting. Both mine and yours. I think we could all be a little better at goal setting." Warren looked out at the faces in the room and they were all staring back at him with blank expressions. The only empathetic face was Roxanne, the training supervisor. Looking directly at her, Warren managed a weak smile and said, "Plus, I'm going to be working on managing progress toward goals too."

The silence in the room was overwhelming and Warren began to wonder if Fran was mistaken. It really did seem like these people didn't like him. "What am I doing wrong?" he wondered. "Why don't they care?"

Of all the things we talk about in *LEAD!*, perhaps this is the most important concept in the book. To be an effective leader, we need to be focused on the other person. Having an "others focused" mindset is a core tenet of Dale Carnegie's leadership model. Dale Carnegie summed it up in principle #17, "Try honestly to see things from the other person's point of view," and principle #18, "Be sympathetic with the other person's ideas and desires."

Leaders serve. That's what they do.

Carnegie Master Trainer Clark Merrill says. "Thinking about the other person is the right mindset. When you get promoted into a leadership position, you need to learn a whole new focus. The truth is, nobody cares about you. It's not that they don't like you, but it's that they want to know, 'What are you going to do as a leader that is going to make me a better person, in my family, at work etc.?' Leaders fail when they lose sight of that. Leaders serve. That's what they do." Clark shares a good technique for making sure that we are in an others-focused state of mind. When you are faced with an issue or problem, ask yourself, "Who are you thinking about?" Ask yourself that. Are you thinking about yourself or the other person? Thinking about the other person is the right mindset. Recognize that even while you're talking, people are thinking about "The WIIFM." What's In It for Me (the listener)?

Qualities of the Others-Focused Leader

What are our qualities when we are others-focused?
- Inspiring
- Develops others
- Positively influences others
- Communicates effectively
- Fosters teamwork, collaboration, and employee engagement
- Facilitates change
- Works cooperatively
- Provides direction

Let's look a little more closely at each of these.

To be *inspiring* is to "breathe life" into another. It's different from motivation, which can be related to the promise of some reward. When we inspire we energize others not for what we can give them, but who we are as a person. Sheryl Sandberg inspired millions of women with her advice to *Lean In*, the title of her best-selling book, and the approach she took to running Facebook as its Chief Operating Officer.

When we *develop others,* we are concerned about the other person's development as a whole. It's not necessarily about developing skills that benefit us in some way, but is a deeper understanding that people have an innate desire to develop and grow. It's about their wants and desires and how we can help them achieve their own goals. Indra Nooyi, the former Pepsico CEO, advises all leaders to "help others rise" as one of her three key leadership lessons. This approach has the mutual benefit of growing the capabilities of the team (which reflects well on their leader) as well as building the individual for their successful future.

When we *positively influence others,* as opposed to telling them what to do based on our title, the changes are often more long lasting and beneficial. When an account manager came into the office of his boss, Lisa Hamilton and told her that he was so frustrated working with his client that he wanted to be reassigned, Lisa didn't tell him to get back to work. She inspired him by saying, "Well, if that's what you want, we'll make that happen. I just thought you were up to the challenge of working with that client. I'll just have to find someone else with more talent." Lisa used Dale Carnegie's principle #21 to "Throw down a challenge," and Hayden, the account manager, took on the challenge and made the relationship work.

All leaders communicate, but when a leader is focused on being heard and understood as well as listening to others and linking the listening to ensuring that they are heard, then the *communication is effective.*

Different Types of Listeners*

Dr. Porter was lecturing to his college freshman business psychology class one afternoon when he began to suspect that they weren't really listening to him. He was outlining his classic theory of motivation and decided to ask them some questions to shake things up.

Brad looked like he would rather be elsewhere. He was sitting there tapping his foot, watching the clock, and checking his phone every minute or so. "Mr. Lawson. This model says that the value of a reward is part of what motivates a person's behavior. Would you agree?"

"Uhhh, yeah. Sure." Brad answered, never taking his eyes off his phone.

Melanie was sitting at her desk, and just kind of staring off into space. Dr. Porter walked over to the window that she was gazing out and stood directly in her line of sight. "Ms. Griffin. The next element of the model says that motivation is influenced by the amount of effort spent. What do you think about that?"

Being spoken to shocked Melanie out of her daydream. "What? I'm sorry, I didn't hear you."

---

* Excerpted from *Listen! The Art of Effective Communication* by Dale Carnegie & Associates.

"What I was saying," Dr. Porter continued, "is that motivation is a factor of several things. Whether the reward is valuable, the eff . . ."

Suddenly Breanna interrupted. "It's the effort spent and the probability of getting the reward." She leaned back and smiled.

Dr. Porter then asked the girl next to her, "Ms. Brenner, what do you find rewarding enough to expend effort for?"

Caitlyn just looked blankly at him through her thickly made up eyelashes. "Nothing."

Next to her, Danny mumbled, "No wonder. You emo types don't care about anything."

Dr. Porter walked over to Danny's desk. "Well, then, Mr. Valdez, what do you find rewarding."

"Sleep. Because that's what this class makes me feel like doing."

Then, Gene piped in. "What seems to be going on here, actually, is that Breanna finds it intrinsically rewarding to demonstrate her knowledge in class, yet also believes that if the professor is aware of her understanding she will earn a better grade in the class. Danny, on the other hand, doesn't feel that he has the ability to succeed in the class so he masks it with an attitude of hostility."

In the back row of the class was a quiet girl, Anna. She shyly raised her hand. "Dr. Porter? You created this model with your colleague Dr. Lawler, right? How did you come to expand on the classic Vroom expectancy theory?"

Dr. Porter smiled and walked back to the front of the room. At least SOMEONE was listening. "That's right,

Ms. Patel. Ed and I took Victor Vroom's theory of expectancy and introduced additional aspects to it. Let's look at this diagram . . ."

Seven Types of Listeners

How many times have you been talking and encountered someone like the students in Dr. Porter's class? How many times have you actually BEEN one of those listeners?

The above scenario illustrates the seven types of listeners identified by Dale Carnegie Training.
- The "Preoccupieds"
- The "Out-to-Lunchers"
- The "Interrupters"
- The "Whatevers"
- The "Combatives"
- The "Analysts"
- The "Engagers"

The first six types are less effective than the seventh. Here is a more in-depth description of each of the types.

The "Preoccupieds"
Brad was a classic "Preoccupied." Tapping his foot and looking at the clock gives the speaker the impression that he isn't giving his full attention. These people come across as rushed and are constantly looking around or doing something else. Also known as multi-taskers, these people cannot sit still and listen.

The "Out-to-Lunchers"

In the above scenario, Melanie was an "Out to Luncher." Dr. Porter was talking, yet she was daydreaming instead of listening. These people are physically there for you, yet mentally they are not. You can tell this by the blank look on their faces. They are either daydreaming or thinking about something else entirely.

The "Interrupters"

Breanna is an "Interrupter." She was just waiting for her chance to jump in and speak. These people are ready to chime in at any given time. They are perched and ready for a break to complete your sentence for you. They are not listening to you. They are focused on trying to guess what you will say and what they want to say.

The "Whatevers"

Caitlyn is a classic "Whatever." Even if she isn't actually using the word, her body language and demeanor gave Dr. Porter the feeling she didn't care about what he was saying at all. These people remain aloof and show little emotion when listening. They do not seem to care about anything you have to say.

The "Combatives"

It's pretty clear that Danny was a "Combative." Hostile and rude, the Combative listener isn't listening for understanding. He or she is listening to get ammunition to use against you. These people are armed and ready for war. They enjoy disagreeing and blaming others.

The "Analysts"

Gene is an analyst. He probably has no idea that his listening style is ineffective. These people are constantly in the role of counselor or therapist, and they are ready to provide you with unsolicited answers. They think they are great listeners and love to help. They are constantly in an analyze-what-you-are-saying-and-fix-it mode.

The "Engagers"

Finally, Anna is an example of an "Engager." These are the consciously aware listeners. They listen with their eyes, ears, and hearts and try to put themselves in the speaker's shoes. This is listening at the highest level. Their listening skills encourage you to continue talking and give you the opportunity to discover your own solutions and let your ideas unfold.

No one can be an engaged listener all the time.

As a leader, listening is critical. As much as we want to be engaged all the time, we fall into the other categories during conversations. Which type of leader are you more likely to be when you're not engaged? Our awareness of what happens when we disengage can help us manage our listening by recognizing when we slip into another pattern. Remember the importance of self-awareness?

Can You Hear Me Now?

What about when we're talking to others? Although it can be challenging to try and communicate with several of these types, there are some things we can do to get through to them. Here are some tips on how to speak to each of the types.

The "Preoccupieds"

If we are speaking to a "Preoccupied" listener, we might ask, "Is this a good time?" or say, "I need your undivided attention for just a moment." We should begin with a statement that will get their attention, be brief, and get to the bottom line quickly because their attention span is short.

The "Out-to-Lunchers"

If we are speaking to an "Out-to-Luncher," check in with them every now and again and ask if they understood what we were saying. As with the "Preoccupieds," we can begin with a statement that will catch their attention and be concise and to the point, because their attention span is also short.

The "Interrupters"

If we are speaking to an "Interrupter," when they chime in, stop immediately and let them talk, or they will never listen to us. When they are done, we might acknowledge their comment and then say, "As I was saying before…" to bring their interruption to their attention.

The "Whatevers"

If we are speaking to a "Whatever," dramatize your ideas (Dale Carnegie's Principle #20) and ask your listener questions to maintain their involvement. Principle #25 applies here, "Ask questions instead of giving direct orders."

The "Combatives"
If we are speaking to a "Combative," when he or she disagrees or points the blame, look forward instead of back. Talk about how we might agree to disagree or about what can be done differently next time. Principle #10 says that "the only way to get the best of an argument is to avoid it," especially when we're trying to gain cooperation.

The "Analysts"
If we are speaking to an "Analyst," we might begin by saying, "I just need to run something by you. I'm not looking for any advice." This helps them to shut off their tendency to offer advice and listen to the conversation so that they can understand what we are saying, rather than listen so that they can fix the problem for us.

The "Engagers"
If you are speaking to an "Engager," take the time to acknowledge their attentiveness. Thank them for their interest in you and your topic. Leaders make a point of acknowledging the positive behavior that works as a strategy to let people know what they should continue to do. Only pointing out what's not working puts people on the defensive and demotivates them. Letting them know what they're doing right reinforces the behavior and motivates them.

What If It's YOU?

Perhaps you recognized yourself in one or more of the types. No need to worry at all! No one is an Engager all of the time. Here are some tips for what to do when we catch ourselves in one of the less effective listening types.

The "Preoccupieds"
If you are a "Preoccupied" listener, make a point to set aside what you are doing when someone is speaking to you.

The "Out-to-Lunchers"
If you are an "Out-to-Luncher," act like a good listener. Be alert, maintain eye contact, lean forward, and show interest by asking questions. This will shift your mindset and improve your focus on the speaker.

The "Interrupters"
If you are an "Interrupter," make a point to apologize every time you catch yourself interrupting. This will make you more conscious of it.

The "Whatevers"
If you are a "Whatever," concentrate on the full message, not just the verbal message. Make a point to listen with your eyes, ears, and heart. Pay attention to body language and try to understand why this person wants to talk to you about this issue.

The "Combatives"
If you are a "Combative," make an effort to put yourself in the speaker's shoes and understand, accept, and find merit in another's point of view.

The "Analysts"
If you are an "Analyst," relax and understand that not everyone is looking for an answer, solution, or advice. Some people just like bouncing ideas off other people because it helps them see the answers more clearly themselves.

The "Engagers"
If you are an "Engager," keep it up. People truly appreciate this about you.

As mentioned, no one can be an engaged listener all of the time. In fact, we all vary from being attentive to what is being said, selective in our focus, and distracted over time. Here's a visual illustration of that.

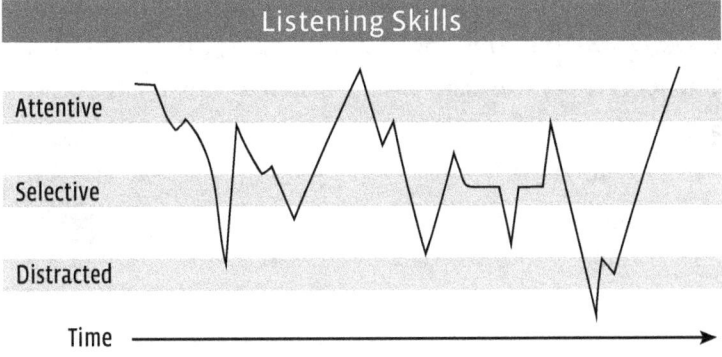

How much time we spend being attentive, selective, and distracted, can vary depending on a lot of factors. What matters is that we learn our personal distractions and when we find our attention wandering, bring it back to the other person using the suggestions above.

Winning the trust of our followers starts with being friendly and likeable. As we've learned, there is no harm in being nice in the workplace, and in fact there are dramatic benefits, since leadership is fundamentally about our relationships with others. Simple courtesies like eye contact and listening, smiling and paying attention to non-verbal cues can go a long way to conveying friendliness. Set the phone down and give the other person your undivided attention. These are the things that make the difference between someone feeling appreciated or unappreciated.

Become a Better Listener

The next principle is to *Become a Better Listener*. It's easy to say, "listen!" and yet another thing to actually do it. In his book *Japan Sales Mastery,* Dr. Greg Story, President of Dale Carnegie Tokyo, offers several concrete tips for becoming a better listener:

1. Stay focused
2. Be patient
3. Interpret both words and emotions
4. Do not interrupt
5. Resist filtering
6. Use humor carefully

7. Summarize the message
8. Wait your turn

Take a picture of this list with your phone, and the next time you find your attention wandering in a meeting, check the list and see what you can do to be more engaged.

The following section is a tool to evaluate your listening skills. Remember what we said earlier about blind spots, too. Consider asking a close friend or colleague to review your answers and discuss them with you to make sure that your self perception is accurate.

Listening Skills Self-Evaluation

Rate yourself on each of the statements using the following scale (Questions 1 through 16):

4 = Rarely   3 = Occasionally   2 = Usually   1 = Always

____ 1. I find that people need to repeat information to me.

____ 2. I experience incidents of miscommunication more than others.

____ 3. I tend to tune people out if their delivery is slow or the material is dry.

____ 4. I find myself finishing sentences for others.

____ 5. I notice customers voice their frustrations with me regarding lack of follow-up or unmet expectations.

____ 6. I steer others away from what they are saying with my questions and comments.

_____ 7. I tend to multi-task when I am listening to other people.
_____ 8. I feel uncomfortable when asking for clarification from the speaker.
_____ 9. When someone comes to me with a problem or challenge, I have the tendency to want to fix it or give advice.
_____ 10. I fake attention.
_____ 11. I form a response in my mind before the speaker finishes.
_____ 12. I need to take notes to remember what is being said.
_____ 13. I make assumptions based on the appearance of the speaker.
_____ 14. I am easily distracted when someone is speaking to me.
_____ 15. I tend to do most of the talking in conversations.
_____ 16. I ask questions that indicate I was not listening.

Rate yourself on each of the statements using the following scale (Questions 17 through 30):
1 = Rarely   2 = Occasionally   3 = Usually   4 = Always
_____ 17. I display an open and accepting attitude toward the speaker.
_____ 18. I am in the loop on important communication at work.
_____ 19. When someone approaches me with a question, I stop what I am doing and give them my complete attention.

_____ 20. I concentrate on what is being said, even if it's of little interest to me.
_____ 21. I listen to the other person's point of view, even if I disagree.
_____ 22. I maintain eye contact with the person speaking.
_____ 23. I try to understand the point of view of people who disagree with me.
_____ 24. I can briefly and accurately summarize what someone else said.
_____ 25. I give the other person a chance to explain fully before responding.
_____ 26. I observe the speaker for nonverbal clues.
_____ 27. I am open to criticism.
_____ 28. I give verbal or nonverbal encouragement to the speaker.
_____ 29. I check to make sure I have interpreted the speaker's message correctly.
_____ 30. I try to "be with" the person speaking by putting myself in his or her shoes.

Listening Skills Scoring

Score yourself in the following manner:

Questions 1–16
Always: 1 point
Usually: 2 points
Occasionally: 3 points
Rarely: 4 points

Questions 17–30
Always: 4 points
Usually: 3 points
Occasionally: 2 points
Rarely: 1 point

Results

105–120 You are a skilled listener. Obtain a second opinion to make sure you have an accurate perception of your listening skills.

95–104 Listening is a top priority for you.

85–94 You listen when it's convenient to you.

75–84 You are an occasional listener.

Below 75 You are brutally honest and have great potential for improvement.

Leadership Isn't About The Leader

As we said in the beginning of this book, leadership isn't about the leader. It's about serving the needs of those being led. In other words, it's about being a person who *fosters teamwork, collaboration,* and *employee engagement.* Phil Jackson, the multiple championship-winning NBA coach says it best, "The strength of the team is each individual member. The strength of each member is the team." Recognizing that we are coaching individuals so that both the individual and the team succeed is critical for our success. To flip a common break-up phrase, when we're the leader, "it's not about me, it's about you."

An others-focused leader *facilitates change* instead of just mandating or implementing it. Change can be hard, and the wise leader facilitates it as a process not an event. Facebook was initially slow to create a platform that works on mobile devices. But once they realized the opportunity, they went all-in on building a platform that would shine on the phone, and they haven't stopped working to optimize it. There was never a time where they said, "okay, we're done with mobile. Now what?" They recognize it as the on-going process that it is, not just a goal to be achieved.

When a leader *works cooperatively* with others, it serves to create a culture and an environment that facilitates working together instead of conflict and turf building.

Finally, an others-focused leader *provides direction*. This doesn't mean telling a follower where to go or how to do their work. Instead "providing direction" means assisting when needed and sharing a powerful vision of where the group is going.

Joe Cardiello, Master Trainer and Director of Training at Dale Carnegie Training Southeast Florida has a very personal example of that. He says, "To be honest, I took Dale Carnegie Training because my mother made me do it. We were in a family business and while I was great at my job, I lacked skills on the people side of things. Fortunately, my mom gave me the feedback I needed to hear and I went to the training. Once I learned how to deal with people, it all clicked. I ended up running and growing our family business. Then we sold it and I came to Dale Carnegie Training and now teach people all over that relationships are the key to everything."

He goes on to say. "You have to focus on people. A lot of in-house training engineers and scientists focus on tasks and work. It's not about the work, it's inspiring people to do their best work. What's your relationship with the people involved? What if the behaviors that you displayed were as if they were your best friend at work? When we get to the root cause of our success as leaders, it's the relationships.

When people are promoted, the best sales people become the worst sales managers. The best engineer becomes the worst manager. Why? Because they're not taught leadership. They rely too heavily on their ability to do the task. And that's not the job of a leader." Remember, being a leader is about getting work done through and with other people.

"If you want to see these principles in action, look at college juniors and their digital communication. They open their devices and go online and onto social media. What is that about? Them. Their opinions. Their ideas. What they think about what you do.

"Instead, we need to look at our behaviors and ask questions instead. The best way to deal with people is to ask questions about them instead of treating them as if they were the stereotype."

Mark Marone, Director of Research and Thought Leadership for Dale Carnegie identified twelve questions to help you uncover the professional hopes and dreams of your employees while understanding and appreciating who they are as individuals:[*]

1. Of all the tasks you undertake in a week or a month, what really makes you feel energized?
2. Do you have any work where you find yourself so engrossed in it that you lose track of time?
3. If you could fill your whole week with work you enjoy doing, what would your week look like?

---

[*] https://www.dalecarnegie.com/blog/12-questions-for-authentic-conversations/

4. What kind of tasks are on your "to do" list when you find yourself procrastinating?
5. Are you doing work that you wish I'd assign to someone else?
6. What parts of your job are you really good at doing?
7. Which parts do you feel you struggle with?
8. If you think about the work you do on a weekly or monthly basis, what are the top five things you do?
9. What do you like most—and least—about the work you do currently?
10. If you could have any job in the company, what would it be?
11. If you could have any job in the world, what would it be?
12. Is there anything holding you back from reaching your goals?

Provides Direction

One of the hardest things an emerging leader can face is learning how to be directive with others. The reason is that we frequently associate "providing direction" with "micromanaging." In reality, the more clear we are in giving direction, the more freedom our direct reports have in accomplishing a task. This is accomplished in both scheduled one-on-ones and the chance encounters we find in a day. In our example of Warren Cantel, he can demonstrate the quality of being others-focused in how he provides clear direction to his team during meetings, and one-on-ones. But he can also do it by noticing the behaviors he wants to see more of and acknowledging it. "Eric, you've been doing a great job of getting those department time sheets in ahead of time. I really appreciate it."

The idea of being others-focused relates directly to several of Dale Carnegie's Human Relations Principles.

4. Become genuinely interested in other people.
7. Be a good listener. Encourage others to talk about themselves.
8. Talk in terms of the other person's interests
11. Show respect for others' opinions—never say "you're wrong."
12. If you're wrong admit it quickly and emphatically.
13. Begin in friendly way.
15. Let the other person do a great deal of the talking.
16. Let the other person feel the idea is his or hers.
17. Try honestly to see things from the other person's point of view.
18. Be sympathetic with the other person's ideas and desires.
22. Begin with praise and honest appreciation.
25. Ask questions instead of giving direct orders.
26. Let the other person save face.
28. Give the other person a fine reputation to live up to.

In this chapter, we talked about the quality of being others focused. Next let's look at the final quality that leads to being a role model. Being strategic.

Key Takeaways

- Having an "others focused" mindset is a core tenet of Dale Carnegie's leadership model.
- The qualities of being Others Focused are:
    1. Inspiring
    2. Develops others
    3. Positively influences others
    4. Communicates effectively
    5. Fosters teamwork, collaboration, and employee engagement
    6. Facilitates change
    7. Works cooperatively
    8. Provides direction
- It's not about the leader. Leaders serve those that they lead. That's what they do.
- Asking questions and then listening to the answers is the way to become others-focused.
- The seven types of listeners are: The "Preoccupieds," The "Out-to-Lunchers," The "Interrupters," The "Whatevers," The "Combatives," The "Analysts," and The "Engagers"
- It's ideal to be an "Engager."
- No one can be an engaged listener all of the time. It's important to know our distractions and draw back focus on the other person.

4. BEING STRATEGIC

"What is is that you want, Warren?" Fran added some cream to the coffee she'd just poured. "When it comes to your working relationships with Carl and the rest of your team, what is the end result you're looking for?"

Warren took a sip of his own coffee and thought about it. He and Fran had talked last week about being others-focused. Maybe this was an opportunity to demonstrate what he'd learned. "I think what I want is to be the kind of leader they want. Someone who can inspire them to a better future and solve problems as they come up." Fran's huge smile bolstered Warren. "I want to be the GPS that gets us to our destination."

"Exactly!" Fran leaned back in her chair, smiling. "Well done, Warren. You're saying that you want to be a strategic leader."

While he hadn't thought of it that way, he nodded in agreement. He'd learned in college that strategy is the art of going from A to B. He wanted to be the kind of leader who could get them there. "Okay, so how do I do that?"

See Through to the Other Side of the Board

In martial arts, karate specifically, the art of *tameshiwari* is the act of breaking items with one's bare hands, feet, or even the head. This dramatic display of focus and strength is a hallmark of what most people think of when they think of karate.

While Dale Carnegie Training isn't recommending that anyone go and try to break boards in half, the practice of *tameshiwari* has several principles that apply to leadership. In order to effectively break a board, for example, several mental steps must precede the action.

First, we must *commit to the action* fully and completely. If we "pull the punch" back halfway through, we're more likely to get injured and less likely to successfully break the board.

Second, we must have *absolute confidence in our ability to succeed*. Whether we believe we *can* do it or we believe we *can't* do it, most likely we will be right. *Tameshiwari* is all about having the guts to mentally commit—not allowing doubt to enter our brain for even a split second. Hesitate and our health could be in *serious* trouble, because something has to break.

Finally, we have to see through to the other side of the board. Don't focus on the board; focus our mind and eyes on what lies on the other side. Then, when we take swift action, that's where our fist ends up.

You Have To Put Your Attention To Where You Want To Go, Not Where You Don't Want To Go.

As a leader, we want to keep our eyes on the end goal, and then guide others there.

To use another analogy, when someone is racing cars, the car goes where their eyes and focus go. If they're focused on a wall they're trying to avoid, the car goes to the wall. We have to be more strategic, and put our attention where we want to go, not where we don't want to go. Hockey great Wayne Gretzky famously said, "I go where the puck is going, not where it has been." Focus matters.

This chapter is not as much about the strategic direction of the company, but is about the personal leadership quality of being strategic as an emerging leader.

What Are Our Qualities When We Are Strategic?

- Innovative
- Solves problems
- Forward-focused
- Uses authority appropriately

Let's look a little more closely at each of these.

In order to get from where they are to where they need to be, a leader needs to be *innovative*. Growth is rarely linear, and progress requires innovative thinking to make it happen. Too often, people think that innovation means creating a new idea or generating a new product. But ask any successful entrepreneur how much of the success was due to the idea, and you'll likely get an answer that paraphrases Edison's famous quote by saying that "innovation is 1% inspiration with a new idea and 99% perspiration from working incredibly hard in new ways." Ideas are easy and important. The hard work is to actually implement it until it is successful.

Every leader has problems. An effective leader *solves problems* well, and takes responsibility for results. It's important to share credit for things going well and to accept responsibility when mistakes happen. This applies at all levels of the organization, since we can't sit around and wait for our boss to solve our problems. One cleaner at a hospital in Nevada attracted attention by purchasing thirty mops. Her boss thought she might be stealing, so she confronted Harley, the janitor. Harley explained that she was concerned that she might be bringing germs from one room into another when she mopped the floors, so she allocated one mop per room when she cleaned the floors. Harley illustrated taking personal responsibility for solving problems before they occur.

To be *forward-focused* means not dwelling on the past. It's about moving beyond "this is how we've always done things" and breaking past the status-quo. Jonathan

Vehar, an innovation specialist at Dale Carnegie shares that he and his business partner invested money in developing one of the first problem-solving apps for a mobile device. Unfortunately, the mobile device was a Palm Pilot, and the infrastructure of the App Store had not yet been invented, so the idea went nowhere and was a big failure. The lesson from this could have been, "don't create any more apps!" And that lesson would be wrong. Staying focused on the future keeps us from getting stuck in the past.

Finally, a role model *uses authority appropriately*. It can be a fine line between being too harsh and too lenient, but a strong role model works to get it right. Alan Mulally, the former Ford CEO says that we should be "tough on the numbers but gentle on the people," meaning that results are important, but so are people, so we should treat them with respect. Flaunting power, domineering because of title or otherwise treating people like they are less than us is not what leadership is about. Effective leaders recognize when they need to challenge their people to be better and when they need to lift them up. As Indra Nooyi from Pepsico says, "We need to help people rise." And that doesn't happen when we're abusing our authority.

What is a Strategic Leader?

Simply put, strategy is the art of getting from A to B. When your company wants to develop a new product, strategy is the ability to get from the idea phase to a fully executed product.

A leader who embodies a strategic mindset has the ability to balance having a clear vision for the future (being forward focused) with the ability to execute the tasks that will lead him or her to that destination, and to overcome the challenges faced on the way.

Strategic leaders influence followers in two ways—directly and indirectly. Our direct influence comes from the things we do and say ourselves. Indirect influence comes when someone is influenced by the implications of what we do at some later point, such as rewards.

Leaders work to influence, and with influence comes power. With power, we have two options. We can use it to overpower subordinates or to empower them. It depends on our intent, and is related to the "uses authority appropriately" quality.

We've all seen examples of domineering leaders at all levels of the organization who are focused on *their* power and *their* results and *their* title. That may work in the short-term, and it may be important for a lone-wolf. However, the ladder of a wolf-pack recognizes that everyone has a part to play in moving a strategy forward. Effective leaders focus the group on both developing and implementing the strategy to help achieve the next level. And they focus everyone on developing the better plan as resources and conditions change.

The Nine Step Innovation Process

Dale Carnegie Training offers this nine step process for innovation, as articulated by Greg Story, President of Dale Carnegie Tokyo:

Step 1. Visualization

This requires some hard and clear thinking around the "should be," the ideal future we want to achieve.

It sounds simple, but there are many interacting parts in the corporate machine, and we need to visualise how we can get them all working together to achieve the ideal outcome.

Time, cost and quality aspirations are in constant tension. We must be careful what we wish for, because if we choose the wrong target, we will hit it!

Step 2. Fact finding

We determine the "as is" situation, namely our current state, and gather data to establish a starting point. This is a critical step to enable measurement, but also to promote the brainstorming process.

It is very difficult to go from a vision to a quality idea in one bound. We need to gather information and use this as our base to launch forward into idea generation.

Step 3. Problem or opportunity finding

We now know where we are and where we want to be, so why aren't we there already? What is holding us back? This step requires identifying and then prioritising the problems or opportunities facing us. A great way to start powerful questions is "In what way can we . . ."

This prioritization step is critical in busy people's lives. We can't do everything, but we can do the most important thing. We just need to be clear about what that thing is.

Step 4. Idea finding

The aim, the reasons holding us back, and key information about the critical aspects of our business should serve as a foundation for brainstorming the creative ideas we need.

However, there is a caveat we need to apply at this point; we must use Green Light Thinking. This means we are aiming for volume of ideas and not judging the quality of those ideas at this point.

We want a big basket of ideas from which to harvest the best. Even if someone in the group comes up with the most ridiculous, idiotic contribution you have had to suffer, which is an affront to your intelligence, we need to just be quiet.

That crazy idea might provoke a truly creative and usable idea from someone else, so don't kill off suggestions at this stage. Encourage people to write down their ideas before sharing with the group and use a good facilitator to make sure all of those ideas are drawn out.

Step 5. Solution finding

Now we use Red Light Thinking. We become judicial, we make decisions about which among competing ideas is best and we now focus on the quality of each idea.

There are many ways to arrive at this process, be it consensus, voting, criteria method (absolutes versus desirables) or directing. The method chosen will vary from issue to issue, and company culture will play a role.

Step 6. Acceptance finding

Ideas are free, but their execution is usually attached to a cost, and this is when we need to get the decision makers involved. An idea may require a pilot program or simply jumping in with both feet. Regardless, don't bother doing any more work unless senior management is with you on this. Think about who are the people likely to support you and who might resist your efforts. Incorporate these people into your plan.

Step 7. Implementation

Now we put the ideas into action as the execution stage to get from "as is" to "should be." This requires a planning process. It doesn't have to be complicated, but it needs to be written down, have names attached to tasks, and have very firm timelines. Think about what needs to happen, who will be accountable for getting it done, by when it needs to be done, and who needs to be kept up to date on its progress.

Step 8. Follow up

Monitoring that people are doing what they say they are doing is always insightful. Good intentions don't cut it. People must be held accountable for their role or the project begins to drift. Set up follow-up meetings at 30-, 60- and 90-day intervals.

Step 9. Evaluation

If we had a precise starting point and a clear goal, and we have executed the project well, then we are in a good position to make judgments about identifying and assessing the end results.

It sounds simplistic when we read this but sometimes the fuzziness and lack of clarity at the start comes back to haunt us at the end. Constantly ask: Do we continue as is or do we need to modify for further success?

In this first part of *LEAD!*, we've talked about how the personal qualities of the leader are essential to his or her effectiveness. It can be a challenging role to play, but is one that is well worth the effort.

In Part Two of *LEAD!*, we'll look at some specific tools and techniques that are used to bring out the best in other people.

Key Takeaways

- The qualities of a Strategic Leader are:
    1. Innovative
    2. Solves problems
    3. Forward-focused
    4. Uses authority appropriately
- A leader who embodies a strategic mindset has the ability to balance having a clear vision for the future (being forward focused) with the ability to execute the tasks that will lead him or her to that destination, and to overcome the challenges faced on the way.
- Strategic leaders influence followers in two ways—directly and indirectly.
- With power, we have two options. We can use it to overpower subordinates or to empower them. Since we can't do it alone, good leaders empower others to achieve the goal.
- The nine steps of the Innovation Process are: visualization, fact finding, problem or opportunity finding, idea finding, solution finding, acceptance finding, implementation, follow up, and evaluation.

Part Two

Unleashing Leadership in Others: Bringing Out the Best in People

Jack Welch, former chairman and CEO of General Electric, said, "Before you are a leader, success is all about growing yourself. When you become a leader, success is all about growing others."

While the foundation of the Dale Carnegie Model of Leadership Success is role modelling the attributes that we want others to embody, it's not enough to achieve the results we want as a leader or an organization. The second part of being a role model is demonstrating the ability to grow others as leaders themselves.

Let's look at the diagram again (see next page).

Dale Carnegie Model of Leadership Success

Role Model	Apply	Outcomes	Results:
Self-Aware			*Your* Desired Performance Results
Accountability	Human Relations Principles	Trust & Personal Growth	
		Positive Change & Organizational Growth	
Others-Focused		Engagement & Agility	
Strategic	Appropriate Tools & Processes	Common Direction & Innovation	

Once we are intentionally modelling the personal attributes of Self-Awareness, Accountability, acting Others-Focused, and being Strategic, the next area of focus is to Apply the Human Relations Principles outlined by Dale Carnegie in *How to Win Friends and Influence People,* and to use Appropriate Tools and Processes as we teach in our Dale Carnegie Training programs around the world.

Doug Stewart, a Dale Carnegie trainer and sales leader in North Carolina, shared his fundamental approach to coaching participants in Dale Carnegie programs to be more effective as leaders. "As they think about their leadership challenge, I have them review the thirty Dale Carnegie principles and choose one that they are committed to applying to the situation. Then I ask them if they have the courage to apply it. If so, we discuss any challenges they might have in applying the principle." Doug reports that this approach is incredibly successful in helping leaders succeed. And while it might seem simple, the power of the principles is that Dale Carnegie managed to distill centuries of the best thinking and knowledge about people working together into thirty principles. And eighty years after he wrote his book revealing these principles, it is still a best seller because the approach works in a way that is easy to understand and apply.

Part Two of *LEAD!* takes the focus from the inner qualities of the leader and shifts it outward to what it takes to bring out the best in our followers.

5. APPLY HUMAN RELATIONS PRINCIPLES

"Warren, come on in." Fran set aside her work and gestured for Warren to sit across from her. "How was the meeting?"

Warren looked upset as he sat down. "Terrible. Everyone is still arguing and infighting and it's a never ending power struggle." He sighed. "I'm too nice to be an effective leader. Josh Branson never has this problem because everyone is afraid of his temper."

Warren was referring to one of the analysts in another division who was infamous for being a tyrannical leader. Josh Branson had a reputation of just walking away from a conversation when he was done with it, even if the other person was still talking. He'd cut off people in meetings, take phone calls in the middle of presentations, and even mocked others. He'd ended up in Fran's office on many occasions because *his people complained about him, but his behavior never strayed into an actual "fireable" offense.*

Fran shook her head. "You're not too 'nice' to be a leader, Warren. We've been working on you becoming a role model and developing personal leadership skills. And your evaluations show that your direct reports all like you and respect you as a person. I think it's time we branch out a bit and work on how you develop others."

In *How to Win Friends and Influence People,* Dale Carnegie laid out a set of "Human Relations Principles" that are as relevant today as they were when he first wrote them. Learning to use them can completely transform the way we interact with people as a leader, and in all of our relationships.

There are thirty principles in all, and we've divided them into three categories that represent the Leadership Pyramid.

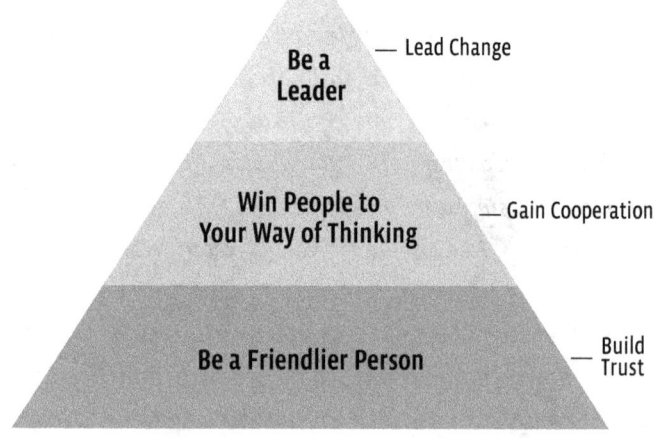

It starts at the base with a focus on becoming a friendlier person, which helps to build trust. The next set of principles focus on how to win people to your way of thinking so we can gain cooperation. The third set of principles focus on things you can do to be a leader, which is critical for leading change.

In the rest of this chapter let's drill down and focus more on each of the three categories.

Build Trust/Be a Friendlier Person Principles 1-9

Paul was a middle manager who was heading up a cross functional product development team. Because the product was being developed by two different groups, he had accountability to two different bosses for this project. It became time to update his bosses on the status of the project and the way his bosses reacted highlight the importance of Principles 1–9. Rather than send a group email or text, which he found to be impersonal, Paul decided to stop into the offices of each of his bosses.

First, he went to Caleb's office and knocked on the door. "Hey, Caleb. Got a minute? I wanted to update you on the progress of the Chiron project."

Caleb didn't even look up but waved his hand motioning for Paul to come in. "Yeah, yeah. I'm just working on something for the division head. Come on in."

Paul came in and sat down in the chair next to Caleb's desk and waited for his attention. Caleb kept looking back and forth between his keyboard and a printout on the desk, and his monitor.

"So, how's it going?" Caleb asked, squinting at the computer screen. "Did you ever work out that scheduling issue with Nancy?"

Paul was aware that he didn't have Caleb's full attention, so he replied, "Yeah, we got that solved. Listen, if this isn't a good time, I can come back . . ."

"No, no. I can do both. So when do you think you'll be starting the prototype phase?"

This wasn't really how Paul wanted to give his update, to a boss who was only half listening and not even looking at him. But he didn't see much choice so he went ahead. "Actually, we are ahead of schedule. Phan has been coming in every day to double check the . . ."

The whole time Paul was talking, Caleb was typing, nodding, saying "uh huh" occasionally and repeating back a few words to let him know that he was listening. But, at the end of the update, as Paul was leaving, he felt disappointed. He had been really excited to share the news about being ahead of schedule, but ended up feeling deflated and underappreciated.

"Next time, I'll just send him an email, even though he'll probably never read it," Paul muttered to himself as he walked down the hall.

As he stopped in front of the other boss's door, Paul took a deep breath and cleared his mind to start again. Knocking on the door and then peeking his head in, he asked, "Omar, do you have a moment?"

Omar turned around in his chair and smiled. "Oh! Paul! Hi, yes, I do. Come on in. I'm just working on a report for the division head. But it can wait. How have you been?"

Paul came in and sat down, relieved that Omar seemed so happy to see him. "I'm doing well, thank you."

"Your daughter was going to sing a big solo in the school concert the other night. How did it go?"

Paul grinned and said, "It was perfect. She was worried about forgetting the words, but she nailed it. I was so proud of her, and she was thrilled at the applause she received from the audience. Thanks for asking." Just then Omar's phone beeped that he had a text. "Do you need to get that? I can wait."

"Oh, no, no. I hate that stupid phone. It's always beeping and bleeping at me. I don't even look at it when I have an actual person in my office. So what's new with Chiron? Rumor has it you guys are ahead of schedule?"

Paul then opened the folder and gave Omar the update, happy that Omar seemed as pleased as Paul was about how hard the team had been working. Paul noticed that Omar kept his attention on Paul while he gave his update, and only interrupted when he had a question about a point that needed clarification. As they started to speak about the next phase of the project, Omar asked Paul about any challenges he might face and what was exciting about it for him.

As the meeting ended, Omar got up and walked Paul to the door and patted him on the shoulder as he walked out. "Thanks so much for the update, Paul. I am really glad to hear how well everything is going and am excited to see the prototype. I appreciate your keeping me updated and in your focus on keeping the team motivated and ahead of schedule. Please tell the team I said to keep up the good work."

Walking down the hall toward his own office, Paul reflected on the difference between the two experiences. One leader came across as indifferent and uncaring. The other conveyed friendliness and interest in the work and in him, which he actually found inspiring.

As you reflect on the conversation between Omar and Paul, notice which of the following principles you noticed Omar using.

Be a Friendlier Person
1. Don't criticize, condemn, or complain.
2. Give honest, sincere appreciation.
3. Arouse in the other person an eager want.
4. Become genuinely interested in other people.
5. Smile.
6. Remember that a person's name is to that person the sweetest and most important sound in any language.
7. Be a good listener. Encourage others to talk about themselves.
8. Talk in terms of the other person's interests.
9. Make the other person feel important—and do it sincerely.

Gain Cooperation/Win People to Your Way of Thinking Principles 10-21

Harvard professor Laura Huang tells a story about the time Elon Musk demanded that she and a colleague leave a meeting*. She and a fellow researcher had gone to hear the business magnate give a commencement address, and had somehow managed to get his contact information and secure a meeting with him. They wanted to talk to him about the challenges of being a startup in the space industry as part of their research.

> By the time the meeting happened, Musk didn't know who the professors were or why they were in his office. She says that within thirty seconds of being in the meeting, he said, "No. Get out of my office." Completely disoriented, she stared at him blankly and asked, "No?" To which he replied, "No."
>
> She continues, "That's when I noticed it: Musk's eyes weren't on us. They were focused on the gift Byron was holding. As it turned out, Musk didn't realize we were academics. He thought we were just two entrepreneurs trying to get his money or endorsement for the company we were presumably starting, and that the gift was our product prototype.

---

* https://www.cnbc.com/2020/02/03/billionaire-elon-musk-told-this-harvard-professor-to-get-out-of-a-meeting.html

The meeting was about to end disastrously—until I did something out of the blue that somehow humored him beyond belief: I giggled. "You think we're trying to pitch you, right? We don't want your money," I told him.

Most people probably would have nodded politely and left, but the giggling gave Musk pause. It wasn't premeditated, nor was it done in a condescending way. It was unexpected. It completely threw him off. And then he started laughing.

"Truth be told," Huang reported, "we crushed the meeting. We chatted, debated, riffed and even hugged each other on our way out. Upon leaving, Musk gave us the contact information of someone who headed up operations for SpaceX to help with our research."

The Leadership Storytelling Formula

This example highlights an important point in leadership. If we can't get people to listen to us, we're not going to have the chance to lead them. We'll get a "no." If they don't even give us the chance to connect with them, you won't be able to win them over to your way of thinking.

What if there were a "secret formula" we could use when speaking to people—whether they are groups or individuals—that would help us instantly connect with them on a personal level? There is. It's called the Dale Carnegie Leadership Storytelling Formula and is a powerfully effective tool in connecting with others. Here is a graph.

Leadership Storytelling Formula
Incident + Insight + Relevance = **Desirable Actions and Results**

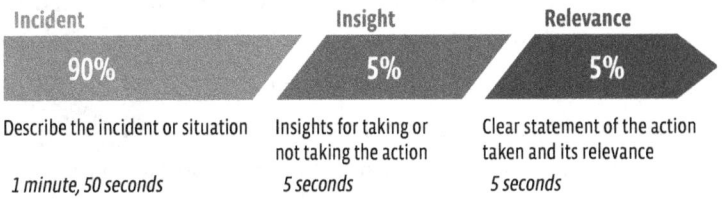

Keys to an Effective Leadership Story
- **Incident**: Describe the situation you faced. Establish who, what, when, where, and why.
- **Insight**: Explain insights for the incident based on taking or not taking the action.
- **Relevance**: Explain what action was taken and the relevance.

One Dale Carnegie student—a school administrator who had spoken with many groups of schoolchildren in the United States and Canada—described the power of storytelling this way: "I quickly learned that in order to keep them interested, I had to tell them stories about people. As soon as I began to generalize and deal with abstract ideas, some little girl would become restless and wiggly in her seat. Then a boy would make a face at somebody. And pretty soon another boy might even throw something across the room." When she told a story, the students were captivated.

When a group of American business executives in Paris signed up for a Dale Carnegie course, their first exercise was a two-minute talk on "How to Succeed." Most of them began by praising various homespun virtues. They preached at, lectured to, and bored their listeners. So the instructor halted the class and said, "We don't want to be lectured to. No one enjoys that. Remember, you have to be passionate and concise. Otherwise nobody's going to care what you're saying. It's that simple. Also remember that one of the most interesting things in the world is honest self-revelation. So tell us where you've been, and who you are—that is what you've earned the right to talk about—because you lived it. Tell us about your successes and your failures. People will gladly listen to that, remember it, and act on it. And by the way, it will actually be much easier for you to deliver than wordy preachments, since you already know it deep inside of you."

In two minutes you can share a short incident that you experienced, and while you're doing this, the audience is fully engaged. You capture their attention with the story in a way that facts, figures, theories, concepts, graphs and charts cannot. Keep the story short and focused on what happened. Be sure that you anchor it in a time and place at the beginning. "Last year, after the board meeting my boss called me into her office . . ." Or "Five years ago I was sitting in the cafeteria across from my colleague . . ." Put us in the scene as quickly as you can without needless preamble like, "Let me tell you a story of a time when my boss was really unhappy with my performance . . ." Jump in, tell the story succinctly in a way that we can experience what you experienced, feel what you felt, and react how you reacted.

Then make sure that the audience understands the point of the story. Tell them your insight, your "aha" moment, your takeaway from the experience. Then provide them with the relevance that answers the question, "so what?" In other words, why are you telling us the story and your insight? How does it relate to the situation or the challenge through which you are leading us?

Here's an example:

> "(INCIDENT) Last year, after the June board meeting my boss called me into her office. I could tell that she was struggling to stay calm. This made me nervous. Suddenly my face felt hot, and I could feel a droplet of sweat run down my spine. She clearly explained behavior that I had manifested in the board meeting that she was not happy with. She pointed out that I had arrived about five minutes after the meeting had started, and I came in with half of a breakfast sandwich in my hand that I finished eating during the meeting. And then on two occasions I interrupted questions being asked by board members in order to defend my initiative. I was embarrassed and ashamed when my boss told me that *she* was embarrassed by my actions. My boss then told me that I needed to improve my professional appearance and demonstrate more respect for the board members if I wanted to stay with the organization. Ouch. (INSIGHT) I realized that I treated the board meeting as just another meeting. What I had done was normal behavior for a regular team meeting, but this was not a regular team. This was the board that provided guidance, support, approvals, and funding for our organization. (RELEVANCE) When we work to understand the various stakeholders or audiences that we work with, it's important to know what is expected of us. If you don't know what is expected of you, ask your boss or a colleague, which may save you some embarrassment or even your job."

Some people wonder how they can tell a full story in less than two minutes. For a good example of how effective brevity can be, think of astronaut Neil Armstrong's famous statement when he first walked on the moon: "That's one small step for a man. . . ." His emphasis was on the everyday physical action. He grounded the moment in something that everyone could relate to. Once he'd done that, the rest of the statement flowed naturally. "One giant leap for mankind" would have seemed preachy and pretentious if he had not first laid the everyday foundation. Armstrong managed to tell a story in only 12 words that echoes around the world to this day.

Win People to Your Way of Thinking
10. The only way to get the best of an argument is to avoid it.
11. Show respect for others' opinions. Never say, "you're wrong."
12. If you're wrong, admit it quickly and emphatically.
13. Begin in friendly way.
14. Get the other person saying, "yes, yes" immediately.
15. Let the other person do a great deal of the talking.
16. Let the other person feel the idea is his or hers.
17. Try honestly to see things from the other person's point of view.
18. Be sympathetic with the other person's ideas and desires.
19. Appeal to the nobler motives.
20. Dramatize your ideas.
21. Throw down a challenge.

Remember that these twelve principles are about gaining cooperation, which is about working together towards the same goal. This is very different from manipulation. The goal here is not to manipulate the other person through deception, false flattery, and lies. It's about the authentic acknowledgment of the other person and what they bring to the conversation. It's not about proving them wrong or creating defensiveness. The point is to work to understand their perspective, and to let them achieve what works best for both of you. Principle 17, "try *honestly* to see things from the other person's point of view," reminds us of the importance of recognizing that to truly cooperate, the goal must be in the interest of both people to achieve the same end. And we do that effectively by honestly engaging with the other person as a full partner in the process.

Lead Change/Be a Leader
Principles 22–30

Holly has been working the front desk reception area for a group of attorneys for five years. Every time a client would come in, she'd engage them and make them feel comfortable because she understood that people don't go to a lawyer unless there's a problem. The lead attorney for the group, Myles, is always great about giving Holly praise in front of the clients. "I don't know what we'd do without her," Myles would often say. "All of our clients absolutely love her and the way she makes them feel welcome." By doing this, Myles and the other attorneys are giving Holly a fine reputation to live up to. This way, if they do need to correct her behavior later on, it is coming from a place of respect. People are much more willing to hear corrective feedback from us when it's not the only thing they ever hear from us. Studies show that the ratio of praise to criticism needs to be anywhere from four-to-one to eight-to-one in order to effectively shift behavior and maintain enthusiasm and morale. This is why the first principle in being a leader is, "Begin with praise and honest appreciation."

Basketball coach Phil Jackson is a perfect example of a leader who demonstrated these principles. Widely considered one of the greatest coaches in the history of the NBA, Jackson was both a competent player (with two championships) and a competent coach (with eleven championship teams to his credit). It was his skill as a player that made him a role model, and his skill as a leader that made him an effective coach.

Phil Jackson coached NBA superstars Michael Jordan, Kobe Bryant, and Shaquille O'Neal. These men were among the most talented players ever to grace the game, but they also had personality traits and interpersonal conflicts that made it hard for them to be coached. In fact, before working with Phil, none of these superstars had ever won an NBA championship.

So, how did he do it? How did Phil Jackson take their diverse skills and challenges and transform these players into a winning team? By realizing that it was his responsibility to bring out the best in each player and then flexing his leadership style to meet the needs of each person.

Michael Jordan, for example, was an incredibly hard worker in the gym. He could push his teammates to go farther through his own example. Kobe Bryant was the same kind of player. Contrast that to Shaq, who had a much more laid back style. He wasn't the hardest worker in the gym and needed to be coached differently. In fact, Coach Jackson recognized that Shaq's attentions were being split between becoming a rap musician and basketball and he threw down a challenge. Stop rapping and you can become league MVP. Shaq did it, and became the league MVP in 2000.

And along the way, they all collected more than their fair share of NBA championships.

This example illustrates the power of supporting one's direct reports in ways that are unique to the person. It's more than just being an effective manager who gives people the information and tools to do their job. It's about recognizing the inherent strengths and weaknesses of each individual and inspiring them to play to their strengths.

> *"In turbulent times like during the Covid pandemic, the whole world is different. But in an important way, it's not different, because people and leaders don't really change. You can only lead on the day you are leading, no matter what is happening. True leadership is like ibuprofen—it knows where to go when you have a headache or knee ache. Open up any page of Dale Carnegie and it will work for whatever ails you."*
> JOE CARDIELLO, MASTER TRAINER AND DIRECTOR OF TRAINING AT DALE CARNEGIE TRAINING OF SOUTHEAST FLORIDA

The Most Prevalent Type of Incompetent Leadership

When looking at the examples above, we can compare this to the different types of incompetent leaders. There's the obvious case where the boss yells at you, demeans you, and basically treats you terribly. This kind of poor leadership is bad enough, but there are more subversive forms.

Laissez faire leadership (leadership where the boss isn't really leading, and lets things just take their natural course) is neither constructive nor destructive. And according to the *British Journal of Management*,* it's the most prevalent type of incompetent leadership in today's business world. This was followed by *supportive disloyal* leadership (or being supportive to your face and then disloyal behind your back), while *tyrannical leadership* behavior was the least prevalent.

What's even worse than having a laissez faire boss? Having an absent one. For many, the idea of having a leader that lets them do what they want sounds ideal. But research** shows that having a boss that ignores you is even worse than having one that treats you poorly.

A 2015 survey of 1000 employees showed that eight of the top nine complaints about leaders concerned behaviors that were *absent*; employees were most concerned about what their bosses *didn't* do. Clearly, from the employee's perspective, absentee leadership is a significant problem,

---

* https://onlinelibrary.wiley.com/doi/abs/10.1111/j.1467-8551.2009.00672.x

** Zeitschrift für Psychologie (2014), 222, pp. 221-232. https://doi.org/10.1027/2151-2604/a000189. © 2014 Hogrefe Publishing.

and it is even more troublesome than other, more overt forms of bad leadership.

What does all of this tell us about how we role model leadership? That a leader will be assessed as competent or incompetent, not by his or her personality or likeability, but how *tangibly supportive he or she is to his or her followers*. Giving followers what they need to succeed, being engaged, and being passionate about leadership is what defines a competent leader in the eyes of followers. What do followers need? The list below of nine principles from Dale Carnegie give us direct actions that help us meet the fundamental needs of those we lead. Of course there are other things too, like clear direction, prompt decisions, salary and so forth. But this is the list that great leaders role model every day.

Be a Leader List

22. Begin with praise and honest appreciation.
23. Call attention to people's mistakes indirectly.
24. Talk about your own mistakes before criticizing the other person.
25. Ask questions, instead of giving direct orders.
26. Let the other person save face.
27. Praise the slightest improvements and praise every improvement. Be "hearty in your approbation and lavish in your praise."
28. Give the other person a fine reputation to live up to.
29. Use encouragement. Make the fault seem easy to correct.
30. Make the other person happy about doing the thing you suggest.

In this chapter we've covered some of the important components of building trust, gaining cooperation, and leading change. We do this by focusing on being a friendlier person ourselves, winning people to our way of thinking, and by being a leader and giving people the support they need. In the next chapter, we'll get into the tools and techniques that we've found are the most beneficial to have as leaders.

Key Takeaways

- Learning to use Dale Carnegie's Human Relations Principles can completely transform the way we interact with people as a leader, and in all of our relationships.
- There are thirty principles in all, and they are divided into three categories that represent the Leadership Pyramid.
- The Leadership Storytelling Formula is this: Incident—90% + Insight—5% + Relevance—5%
- Effective leadership is about recognizing the inherent strengths and weaknesses of each individual and inspiring them to play to their strengths.
- No matter what is happening around us, we can only lead on the day we are leading.

6. USE APPROPRIATE TOOLS AND PROCESSES

"I'd like a large cold brew with oat milk and two pumps of sugar free vanilla, please." It had been three weeks since Fran Bianco had met with Warren Cantel and she was looking forward to hearing how he'd been implementing the tools she'd given him. They were meeting at the in-house coffee place at work for an update.

"Let me get that for you, Fran." Warren came up behind her and handed his credit card to the cashier. *"And to quote a famous movie line, I'll have what she's having."*

They got their coffees and went to sit down. Fran was amazed—it seemed like Warren even LOOKED different.

"So, how's it been going Warren?"

"Much better. As you noted, I already had a lot of the qualities at the bottom of the pyramid. The whole

'be a friendlier person' stuff. I now needed to move up to the 'gain cooperation' level. That was what had been missing."

"Honestly, that's pretty common when you get promoted from within a group. It can be hard to establish leadership with a group that was formerly your peers." Fran took a sip of her coffee. "But, I promoted you because I knew you were up to the job. I'd seen how you managed your former direct reports, and felt confident that you could grow even more as a leader. So, tell me what you've been doing."

"One thing I did was apply the Leadership Storytelling Formula when I was running meetings. So, for example, two Tuesdays ago we had a meeting to go over that new Inclusion Training that we're rolling out next quarter. Before talking with you I'd been dreading it. Everyone was so negative about the specific program I picked, but I knew that they really hadn't read it. So what I did was start the meeting by sharing a story of when I first got a job—not here but at another place—where I was literally harassed because of my accent. I didn't just tell them what happened, but I helped everyone on the team remember how it feels to be excluded for something. After telling the story, I then asked them for one thing. Read the training documents. Just read it with an open mind that this training might help others not feel that horrible feeling of not fitting in."

"Wow, that sounds like a perfect application of The Storytelling Formula. How did it turn out?"

"Everyone on the team did it, except one person. And then last week members of the team shared their stories about how they had felt excluded, which really increased the enthusiasm for the project."

"Warren, that's great!" Fran didn't want to disempower Warren by asking who the one hold-out was, because she didn't want the meeting to turn into *"Warren going to his supervisor to report on the behavior of a direct report."* So she said, *"Okay, don't tell me who isn't on board, but tell me how you handled it."*

"What I did was use the 'giving feedback' stuff you shared with me." Warren leaned forward in his chair, took a sip of his own iced coffee, and continued. *"Before I called the person into my office, I thought about what kind of communicator they were. Should I be more direct, or less direct?"*

Fran nodded. *"Good, good."*

"Then I reflected on the behaviors I didn't want to change, and found a way to compliment them on this before criticizing their behavior. I said, 'I really respect what you bring to the group. You have a clear idea of equity and what's fair, and I value that.' I then mentioned that we needed everyone committed if we were going to be successful, and talked about a time that I'd felt like I had to do things I didn't really want to because I hadn't been part of the decision. Then I told them that, 'one thing that I have noticed, though, is that you tend to jump to what's unfair first in meetings. So when I asked everyone to take a look at the training materials, you immediately rejected the

idea because you felt it wasn't fair that the whole team didn't have input on picking the program I chose.'"

Fran was impressed! This was a fantastic application of what she'd taught him! "So, how did it turn out?"

Warren grinned, "I used my killer listening skills to find out what was at the root of the issue and in the end he agreed to at least look at the training materials and we're going to meet again on Tuesday to talk about it. I just needed to let him know that I was open to choosing a different program if there were solid reasons not to use the one I chose."

"That is really great, Warren. I'm proud of you. Let's drill down a little more now on some additional tools and processes you can use as you continue to grow as a leader."

Leadership Tools and Processes

Let's look at the application of tools and processes that allow you to be an effective leader. This chapter delves into some of the material that we teach in our Dale Carnegie Leadership Training Programs around the world. Thousands of people in virtually every type of organization have learned these tools and processes to become more effective leaders.

The Thinking Mechanism

In our example before, Warren was tasked with choosing an Inclusion Training program for his workplace. Because he unilaterally chose the program and then simply presented his choice to them, he experienced resistance. Ironically, if he had included them in the process of choosing the program, he would have had better buy in.

All it would have taken would have been an understanding of the two kinds of thinking.

As a leader, we are responsible for two basic kinds of thinking. We like to call them "green light" and "red light."

With Green Light Thinking, we are in an uninhibited creative thinking mode. It's not about judging the information, but is instead brainstorming options. It's about the quantity of information gathered, not the quality. Whether conducted in a team setting or on our own, Green Light Thinking is characterized by the rapid generation of many, many ideas.

Once the options have been created and collected, then it's time to shift to Red Light Thinking. This is the evaluation phase where we evaluate our ideas based on their merit. Red Light Thinking follows Green Light Thinking, and the two processes should always be kept separate. If a traffic light is both green and red, we don't know what to do! The same is true with the thinking mechanism in our brains. That's why we need to be deliberate about doing one or the other, but not both at the same time.

One way that Warren could have avoided conflict in the team would be to conduct a green light brainstorming session before choosing a program. By meeting with the team and asking everyone for input on program options, he would have been able to gather a lot of information and ideas. Then later, they would have used Red Light Thinking to evaluate the options. He could have then delegated the task of finding training programs to the team so that they could have chosen the ideal one as a group. This would have built commitment, since people support a world they help create.

The Delegation Process

If leadership is the process of getting things done through others, then task assignment is one way to get things done without doing everything oneself via the process of delegation.

Leaders may choose to delegate for many reasons. Delegating:
- Allows us to shift some of our workload and frees us to work on other tasks.
- Provides an opportunity to develop our people.
- Allows us to take advantage of the specialized skills or preferences of others on our staff.
- Enables us to distribute the workload, thus speeding up the process of getting things done.

Here's the process for delegation:

Identify the need: establish what you choose to delegate and create a picture of the desired outcome.

Select the person: identify to whom you will delegate and what strengths that person has to be successful, or what strength would be enhanced to help them achieve their goals (this sometimes happens before identifying the need).

Plan the delegation method: think about what is the desired outcome of the delegation plan? What is the current reality of the situation? What are the realistic goals that need to be accomplished?

Hold a delegation meeting: Be sure to identify the vision/goals for the person to whom you are delegating. Identify the specific results to be achieved. Outline the rules and limitations, and review the specific standards of performance.

Create a plan of action: The person to whom you delegate should develop a plan of action that explains the steps to be taken, by when they'll be done, and who is responsible for accomplishing them.

Review the plan: Based on the plan they create, review and make any necessary adjustments until you're both in agreement.

Implement the plan: Ensure that all people concerned understand their part in the work, are committed, and act together to put the plan into action.

Follow up: Successful leaders follow-up on the goals and identify deviations from the expected goals. Concentrate on factors that impact the success of the project, and provide corrective action to be taken. Don't wait until the project is complete to follow-up. This should be an ongoing process in support of the person to whom the project has been delegated.

During the Assignment
- Continue to create an environment of empowerment, trust, confidence, development, and support.
- Let the employee drive the action and carry out their responsibilities with minimal interference, but support them when necessary.
- When checking progress, let the employee drive the discussion; do more listening than talking.
- Try to help the employee learn to solve problems and answer questions themselves whenever possible.
- If the employee keeps coming back to you repeatedly with the same questions, explore the situation and try to get some additional feedback. Assess whether or not you are explaining things clearly, if there is a comprehension problem, if there is a confidence problem, or if the employee is in need of further development.

When we assign tasks, we establish in the minds of our team members that they are accountable for delegated results. In every decision, large or small, some risk is involved. This is a reasonable, allowable margin for deviations from performance standards. If there is not such latitude, the employee may conclude that the necessary authority has not been granted to achieve desired results, and they'll feel micromanaged and lose enthusiasm for the project.

Note a subtle difference between "task assignment" and "delegation." The former is about getting things done, but that latter can be a powerful way of helping to develop people. When we're assigning tasks, we're giving it to the best person for the job in order to accomplish a task. But delegation advances the developmental opportunity for the person with whom we're working. In this case, the check-ins may be more like supportive coaching sessions rather than telling people what to do.

"Cameron" was a mid-level manager who was already at full load when her boss asked her to take on a team responsible for implementing a new way of designing products in the organization. Cameron protested that she really didn't want the project. Her boss gently reminded her that she had been asking for more exposure in the organization, and a way to interact more with the other offices around the globe. While this project required some new skills and approaches, with support from her boss Cameron was able to succeed with the team, and embed the new process in the organization. The recognition of her success with this challenging task led to her promotion to a new and bigger role three months later.

Performance and Results

Holding people accountable for their actions can be one of the hardest things for a leader. Especially when they are a "nice guy" like Warren.

Kent Kakaur had just been hired as the General Manager of a hotel in Nashville, Tennessee and his task was to turn the property around. He'd done this earlier in his career, but took a fifteen year hiatus to raise his kids as a stay at home dad. After years of being the "cookie dad" at

Girl Scouts and other "nice guy" stuff, Kent wondered if he still had what it took to turn around a failing hotel.

When he got there, he was shocked at how bad the conditions were. It was no wonder the property was losing money. The lobby was infested with prostitutes and their clients, drug dealers, and everyone had gotten so used to it that the police didn't even come anymore when they called. What was the use, when the riff raff would be back within an hour?

The first thing Kent did was bring each of his staff in to get to know them better. He used a process we teach called The Innerview, which is different from an interview.

The Innerview

Many leaders find that having a deeper connection with their team enhances their ability to create an environment that elicits commitment instead of compliance. Conducting an "Innerview" is a proven method of deepening our connection with our people through a casual conversation.

In this process, the leader converses with his or her team members in a way that generates information and connection. This isn't designed to evaluate or judge the team member, like a traditional interview, but instead simply ask questions for the purpose of understanding commonalities.

Clark Merrill, a Carnegie Master Trainer, shared a story of how powerful the Innerview is. "When I do the Innerview exercise, I have people pair up, and I tell them to find someone of a different generation. In one course, this participant said, 'I don't know why I'm even here, and I'm just going to prove it doesn't work.' So I paired him up with someone completely different than he was. They went through the Innerview questions and in the debrief, I asked him how it went. He was shocked at how well it worked. He said, 'Wow, I can't believe what I just learned. My partner thinks in a whole way I never thought possible. I just took for granted what he would think. I was trying to prove this was a waste of time. However, it tells me when I go back to work I need to talk to my people . . . no, I am going to *listen* to them.' He went back to work and everyone was surprised. They asked him, 'What happened to you?'"

Remember that the Innerview isn't about you asking and the other person answering. This conversation should be a dialogue that engages both of you so that you both learn something and discover commonalities.

Three Types of Innerview Questions
1. Factual questions
These are questions that are typically conversational in nature and revolve around factual information. The answers to these questions are occasionally found in personnel files. Examples of factual questions are:
- Where did you grow up?
- What kind of activities were you involved in as a kid?
- Tell me about your first job.
- What were your interests in school?
- Tell me about your family.
- What do you do for fun?

2. Causative questions

These are questions to determine the motives or causative factors behind some of the answers to the causative questions. They are typically "why" and "what" questions. Examples of causative questions are:
- Why did you pick that particular school?
- What caused you to study that?
- What brought you to your current job?
- What direction did you go in right after high school?
- How did you get involved in that hobby?

3. Values-based questions

These are questions to help connect with a person's values system. They are designed to help a leader hear what a person feels is important. They are also questions that people rarely ask, but give a greater view of the inner person. Examples of values-based questions are:
- Tell me about a person who had a major impact on your life.
- If you had to do it all over again what, if anything, would you do differently?
- If there were a major turning point in your life what might that be?
- There are many highs and lows as you go through life. Are there any of either that had a significant influence on you?
- What words of wisdom would you give a young person if he/she sought your advice?
- How would you sum up your personal philosophy in a sentence or two?

The goal of the Innerview is not to get through all of the questions as quickly as you can, nor is it even to cover all of the questions. The goal is to understand the other person, find commonalities and get to know them as people, not just their job title, role, or responsibilities. Leadership is about relationships. The Innerview helps build that in both directions.

After the Innerview, you are in a much better position to apply the tools and processes needed to lead the individual.

In our example with Kent, he gathered together the staff of the hotel and had a meeting. He used The Leadership Storytelling Formula to establish a vision for what he wanted the hotel to be like, and then gave everyone one task. Get rid of the riff raff. Prostitutes and drug dealers would be asked to leave the premises. Guests who were engaging in that type of behavior would be asked to leave. If someone felt uncomfortable doing this, they could come to Kent for coaching. And if the guest resisted, Kent was more than happy to come and get tough with them himself.

The next night Charley, the night front desk manager, came to Kent. "I want to do it, but I don't know how."

Six Levels of Positive Feedback or Empty Praise vs Solid Praise

There are six levels of positive feedback, which we sometimes call praise. Praise is a "polite expression of admiration." Positive feedback lets someone know what they are doing right—those things we want to ensure that they keep doing—even as they change other behaviors. Praise and feedback help your followers grow and flourish, as long as they perceive it as being sincere and specific to them.

The six levels range from giving feedback about things that are impersonal to those that are very personal.

6. Level of Vision: This is the highest form of compliment, as it is the most global. "You really get the concept of customer service."

5. Level of Identity: These are things that are core to a person. "You are an important member of the engineering team."

4. Level of Belief: These are more internal qualities about the person. "You have a positive outlook."

3. Level of Skills: "You're great with Photoshop."

2. Level of Behavior: Things that are observable. "You did not interrupt when Janet was telling you about the problems with the project."

1. Level of Environment: Things like your car, clothing, home, or office. "I like the new artwork on the wall."

When you are giving feedback, strive to bring up your feedback to a higher level, because the lower levels have less impact than the higher ones. Would you rather be complimented on the color of your shirt or receive positive feedback which acknowledges how well you deliver on the vision. The higher the level of feedback, the more someone feels understood and acknowledged based on who they are, rather than things that are easily visible.

Here are some examples of how it works.

Instead of "Your PowerPoint was very thorough" (environment), try "I really appreciate how you ask other team members questions to engage them in the project" (behavior).

Or "You're really good at organizing things" (skills), becomes "You are a really organized person (identity)." Or even, "You helped all of us be more organized (vision)."

Notice how much more effective the feedback becomes when it is backed up with something you noticed.

Compare:
"You're really responsible"

to
"I like how you remembered to be on time to our meeting even though you were working through that customer issue" (behavior). "You're really responsible" (Identity).

Compare:
"You're a great listener."

to
"You're a great listener (skill). It's a pleasure to have someone of your caliber in our organization" (identity).

Why? A person's identity can only be formed with the proof of what you actually noticed. They will really believe you think he is a responsible person because you pointed out an example of when he was responsible.

Think about how you feel when you get an "empty compliment" such as "You're one great guy!"

As opposed to a "solid compliment" such as "Wow you remembered my work anniversary. You're one thoughtful guy!"

Beware of empty praise /feedback!

Remember earlier when we talked about the *laissez faire* boss who let people do what they want and gave praise that had no substance? We should not tell an employee, "You're the best!" without any specific feedback because it has no meaning. Nor does it reinforce specific behaviors we want to continue to encourage. The best at what? What should they keep doing? Although it is a start and may be better than giving no positive feedback at all, the goal is to be as specific, effective, and believable as possible.

Another trap is telling an employee who is really not helpful that he is wonderful. People can tell how we really feel about them, and if we give false praise it leads to dissonance. "I'm getting terrible performance evaluations, but she's telling me how great I'm doing."

When we can't find anything to praise we need to dig deeper. Even behavior that is expected can be genuinely acknowledged. "I appreciate that you're here every morning ready to work the phones."

How to Give Coaching to Higher Levels of Performance

This isn't to suggest that the only kind of feedback we should give is positive. There is an art to giving constructive feedback but it is an important part of the feedback loop. As Dale Carnegie stated, it's best to call attention to the person's mistake indirectly (principle #23) and to start with one of your own (principle #24).

Edgar and Erika

Let's say you have two employees, Edgar and Erika. You gave them a project to work on, but instead of doing it in a timely manner, they have been putting it off.

Because people are different, we can't necessarily give them feedback in the same way. Here's an example.

You call Edgar in first. He's a direct communicator. If we talk too long or go into a lecture mode, we'll see his eyes glaze over. If we aren't direct enough, he won't hear us.

"Edgar. I really appreciated yesterday when you helped Kurt with the problem he had with his computer. That was really helpful. But I am still waiting for you and Erika to send me that information I asked you for a couple of weeks ago. Usually you get right on those kinds of projects and I would appreciate it if you focused more on the tasks I give you before helping other people."

All Edgar heard was "I was helpful yesterday. In the future she wants me to do those projects earlier." He's not going to hear that we need him to get the project done immediately.

So, we decide not to make the same mistake with Erika. We call her in. "Erika. I was wondering where that information is that I asked you and Edgar for a couple of weeks ago. It's irresponsible of you to take so long."

Erika is an indirect communicator and is likely to be so upset that she has disappointed us that she is overwhelmed. The feedback is too direct. She may sit in front of her computer but she's likely to be too upset with herself to perform effectively. So how can we provide better developmental feedback? This is where the Dale Carnegie Coaching Process comes in. The following graphic illustrates the connection between the process and Dale Carnegie's Human Relations Principles.

The Dale Carnegie Coaching Process

The Coaching Process

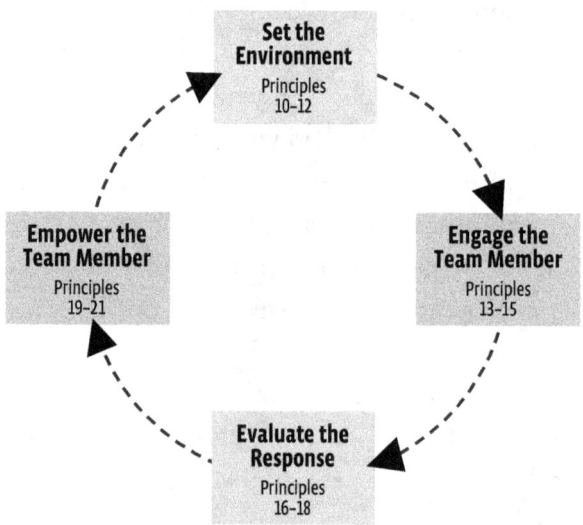

Step One. Set the environment (principles 10–12)

Make sure the team member you are coaching is open to the coaching process. We should avoid blaming them and we should demonstrate our respect for them, and if appropriate share stories of when we struggled with the same thing.

Step Two. Engage the team member (principles 13–15)

A good coach helps team members discover opportunities for improvement and realize they can do it by themselves. Getting agreement and having team members express their ideas will engage them in the process.

Step Three. Evaluate the response (principles 16–18)

Ideally, the team member starts "owning" the idea. The coach should evaluate what the team member says and work to see things from the team member's perspective and be sympathetic with his or her situation to build the ground for the next step.

Step Four. Empower the team member (principles 10–12)

During this final step the team member will start taking action. He or she needs to be encouraged by a strong "why" and/or a challenge.

In Kent's example, he listened to the front desk manager and what the experience had been like up to this point. Kent shared with him some relevant stories of when he was the GM at a hotel in Las Vegas and how scared he was at first to confront the undesirable elements that came into the hotel (Step One). He then shared some strategies that worked for him, and asked the manager what he thought of those ideas (Step Two). They talked about some of the things that had been tried before, and Kent expressed sympathy with his perspective (Step Three). It was then time for the manager to try it himself, and so with Kent watching, the manager went over to a group of people who were loitering in the lobby and asked them to leave. Kent then challenged the manager to do this every night for a week and report back to him how it worked (Step Four).

Supporting Peak Performance

Of course performance is never linear. Sometimes, despite our best efforts, people don't perform as expected. Some of Warren Cantel's team won't read the materials requested. Some of Kent's hotel employees will continue to look the other way from unruly guests.

What are some reasons that even when employees are crystal clear about goals and expectations, they may "miss the mark" in terms of their performance/output?

Here are some categories of reasons.
- People lack necessary skills and knowledge.
- People lack the resources they need.
- There are rewards for undesirable performance.
- There are no consequences for desired performance.

In Kent's case, his people hadn't had the necessary skills to deal with such extreme behavior in the workplace. They were scared and didn't know what to do. So he gave them the resources they needed. And, until now, there had been no consequences for doing it, and the rewards for not doing it were that the employees could just "look the other way" and still keep their jobs.

Reasonable Allowable Margin of Error

As a leader or a coach, expecting perfection will lead to disappointment. Just as when you're driving, you don't always stay exactly within the lines of the road. Sometimes you veer to avoid something. Sometimes you go just outside the lanes when you're changing the music. It happens, and as long as you don't hit the guardrails or another car, it's okay. Similarly, if the team member has deviations within the lines, those are opportunities for coaching. But if he or she strays outside the lines consistently (or hits a guardrail), those are obvious performance deviations. How can you tell whether subpar performance is a coaching issue or is something more?

Evaluating Subpar Performance

When someone who seems to have the capability to do the work is not performing to expectations, answer the following questions:
- What questions should you ask yourself to evaluate your own impact on the situation?
- What else should you ask to evaluate the situation? (This may include other variables besides your own impact.)
- What should you try to observe in the workplace?
- How can you avoid making assumptions?

In other words, first look at yourself. What is your role in their subpar performance? Have you done your part in clearly conveying expectations? If the answer is yes, it's time to look somewhere else. Is there something else going on with the employee? Maybe some personal issue that you don't know about? Bring them in and talk to them. Don't assume that the sub par performance is intentional or is a result of a "bad attitude."

Randah had been working with her team for three days and three nights to get a proposal submitted to a prospective client. It had been a lot of work and it required many late hours, but the proposal was submitted in time and—if accepted—would help them achieve their goals. When Randah's boss saw the proposal he was upset by the typos and some inconsistent formatting. He scheduled a meeting with the team because he was so disappointed at what he saw as poor quality and intended to chide them. Before the meeting, Randah reminded the boss that the team had worked practically non-stop to get the proposal completed, and had done everything possible, given the client's short timeline, to ensure the most perfect proposal possible. Since the boss wasn't aware of this, he shifted his approach to the meeting by starting with sincere praise and appreciation, and then asked the team to debrief what worked and what could be improved next time. During the conversation, the team suggested that next time, they needed to bring in someone from outside the team to review the proposal before they sent it out to ensure a better quality final proposal. The boss and the team left the meeting satisfied that the team's hard work had been recognized, and that they would do better next time.

Framework for Handling Performance Deviations (Principles #22-30)

Dale Carnegie Training has developed an effective framework for handling performance deviations. It looks like this:

Framework for Handling Performance Deviations

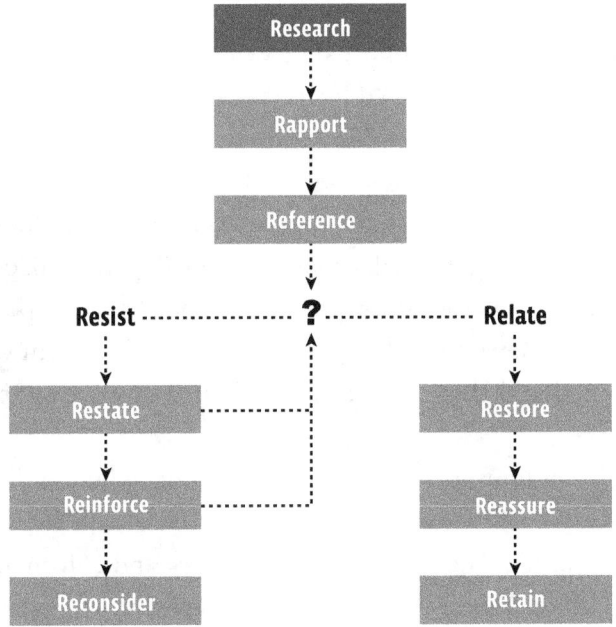

Research

Do the homework to make sure you have all the facts before you meet. Don't build a case, but gather information. Also, try to keep an open mind and look beyond the facts to better understand motivations. Research starts with the question, "Is the person worth saving?" Your answer defines your next move.

Begin With Rapport

Rapport is a reservoir of goodwill and mutual trust accumulated over a long period of fair treatment (the Innerview we discussed earlier helps fill that reservoir). When meeting with the person, begin by putting them at ease and reducing their anxiety. One way to do this is to begin with honest appreciation that is supported by evidence. Choose a behavior that you have observed instead of giving a compliment.

Reference the Performance Deviation or Issue

During this step focus on the problem and not the person. Eliminate personal pronouns and depersonalize the problem. It was the action that was wrong, not the person who did it. Give the other person a chance to explain what happened and then inform them of what you know about the issue.

Listen to understand and determine whether he or she is accepting responsibility or blaming and avoiding responsibility. The goal is to gather facts and information to accurately identify the problem and why it happened. By reducing defensiveness and not jumping to conclusions, different perspectives surface and the root cause of the problem can be identified.

The moment of truth is when the person will either **relate** to the problem or **resist** in some way. Their actions, attitude, and behavior in this decision will determine your next move.

When the person **relates** to the problem, issue, or performance deviation, and takes responsibility, move to the next step.

Restore Performance

The purpose of this step is to remedy the problem, to reduce the chance of the issue happening again, and to restore the person's performance. It also involves devising a way to keep the problem from occurring again.

This step is handled differently with the employee who accepts responsibility than with the one who blames and avoids taking responsibility. With the responsible employee, coaching is used to encourage him or her to suggest ways to correct the situation. The employee can be involved in a problem analysis and decision making process. For the blaming or avoiding employee, first reaffirm performance expectation and then coach acceptance of responsibility to restore accountability.

Reassure

This step is focused on the person. Obviously a person who has erred feels, to some degree, like a failure and is likely to be less inclined to approach the next opportunity with confidence. Therefore, the leader helps the employee see the situation in a different context.

Assure the employee of his or her value and importance to the organization and that he or she has your support and encouragement. The employee should leave the meeting feeling motivated to achieve optimal performance because he or she has a solid relationship with the organization.

The goal for the blaming or avoiding employee is to leave with a sense of accountability and an understanding or the organization's expectations. The employee should also understand that you are interested in, and committed to, their success and growth.

Retain

If you handled the previous steps well, you increased your chances of retaining the person, his or her commitment, and the morale of your whole team. This builds trust and increases the level of commitment and work ethic.

When people **resist** your efforts to repair the situation or performance, or refuse to relate to the issue, then we need to move to the Restate step.

Restate

You now restate the facts, the seriousness, the policy, and the proper remedy to the issue. This gives the person one more chance to do the right thing.

Reinforce

When people refuse to accept responsibility, you may have to formally remind them in some way prior to further action. There may be policies and procedures documented in your organization for this.

Reconsider

Sometimes you find that the employee is not a good fit for a particular task, project, or department. You may explore what the employee's strengths, interests, and goals are and search for a better fit within the organization. It is an injustice to employees and organizations to perpetuate a situation where individuals feel that they can never succeed. The last resort—after attempts to coach them for desired performance—is to remove them from this area of responsibility; to replace, reassign, or release them from the organization.

Example of the Framework for Handling Performance Deviations in Action

"Thanks for coming in, Carl." Warren Cantel *greeted the man as he entered the office. "Have a seat." He'd done his* **research** *before the meeting and was ready to address Carl's performance issue. First, it was time to build rapport. "How is your wife liking that new car of hers? What was it again . . . a Honda?"*

"She likes it a lot, really. I keep asking her if I can use it, but she always conveniently has somewhere else to go when I want to borrow it." He laughed and Warren nodded in agreement. "Just tell her you'll take the kids to soccer. She'll be happy to let you drive it then."

"You got that right." Carl's tense shoulders began to relax. It was time to **reference the problem**.

"So, I wanted to talk to you about the job description thing. What's been going on with that?" Warren then paused to let Carl explain.

"Yeah. So the thing is, it's way harder than we thought it was going to be. Some of these job descriptions haven't been updated since the eighties and they don't use inclusive lan-

guage. I'm having to do a lot of research to make sure I'm using the proper terminology." Since Carl was relating to the problem instead of getting defensive, Warren felt that they'd gotten to the root of the issue.

"Oh that makes sense. We really are up against a tight timeline, though. How can I help you get them done this week? What do you need from me to make that happen?" He was eager to help **restore performance**.

"I feel really bad about this, Warren. I don't know. Maybe if we got Leah to help me? She's a whiz at these compliance issues."

Warren was glad to hear that Carl felt bad for missing the deadlines. Now he needed to **reassure and retain** him. "I appreciate that, Carl. You really have been putting in extra time on this that I had no idea was happening. It should be no problem to get Leah in to help you."

"So what we'll do then is get Leah to help you go through the job descriptions to make sure they are all compliant and use inclusive language and you guys can get them to me by Monday. Does that sound good?" He was glad he only needed to restate the issue and not reconsider Carl's entire future on the team.

Carl smiled and looked genuinely relieved. "That sounds great, Warren. Thank you."

In this chapter we talked about the tools an emerging leader can use to coach and lead employees to higher levels of performance.

Key Takeaways

- There are two kinds of thinking: Green Light and Red Light.
- Green Light is uninhibited creative thinking mode. It's not about elimination options, it's about generating them.
- Red Light is the evaluation mode. This is the discerning phase where you evaluate your ideas based on their merit.
- Leaders may choose to assign tasks for many reasons.
  - —Allows us to shift some of our workload and frees us to work on other tasks.
  - —Provides an opportunity to develop our people.
  - —Allows us to take advantage of the specialized skills or preferences of others on our staff.
  - —Enables us to distribute the workload, thus speeding up the process of getting things done.
- Here's the process for delegation:
  - —Identify the need
  - —Select the person
  - —Plan the delegation method
  - —Hold a delegation meeting
  - —Create a plan of action
  - —Review the plan
  - —Implement the plan
  - —Follow up

- The "Innerview" is a proven method of deepening our connection with our people through an informal conversation focused on discovering commonalities.
- The six levels of positive feedback are:
    - —Environment
    - —Behavior
    - —Skills
    - —Belief
    - —Identity
    - —Vision
- See the effective framework for handling performance deviations on page 145.

In Part One of the Dale Carnegie Model of Leadership, we looked at the personal leadership qualities that allow us to role model what we want to see in others: Self-Awareness, Accountability, Focus on Others, and Being Strategic.

In Part Two of the Dale Carnegie Model of Leadership, we covered the second part of being a role model—the application of the Human Relations Principles and the use of Appropriate Tools and Processes in leading individuals and groups.

In Part Three, we begin to look at how everything we've learned to this point leads to the outcomes desired, so that when we put all three parts together, we can achieve the individual and organizational goals that are most important to us.

Part Three

Unleashing Desired Outcomes

Amazon. Google. Facebook. Uber. Those are just a few of the companies that are considered "industry disrupters." They redefined, or in some cases defined, the way business is done in their industry.

But just as McDonald's and Walmart before them; when a company changes the face of business, is it the company who is driving the change? Or is it the leaders?

At Dale Carnegie Training, we believe that it is the leaders of an organization who drive the company in a direction that makes others want to follow. Companies are made up of people, and it's people who are the leaders.

This book wasn't written for the executive teams of Amazon, Google, Facebook or Uber, though. It was written for the developing leader in the organization who wants to be able to achieve the outcomes that will support the goals of the organization. For every Jeff Bezos, Sundar

Pichai, Mark Zuckerberg, and Dara Khosroshahi there are thousands of leaders who work *for* them whose work helps achieve the company's goals. Similarly, you may not be the top leader in your organization, but the projects that you lead are important for the success of the organization.

That's why the foundation we lay out in this book, and in our Leadership Success Model is that of personal leadership. It's your value as a leader that allows you to influence the people around you and achieve the results that affect the success of the company.

Let's look at our model again, and how the ideas we've explored in the book lead to leadership outcomes.

Dale Carnegie Model of Leadership Success

A certain set of outcomes emerge as an individual leader role models leadership behaviors, develops his or her personal leadership skills, and applies the Human Relations Principles along with the tools and processes to develop new leaders. The results of those outcomes are the performance results that are our goals. But before we can achieve those results, we need to achieve the outcomes of trust and personal growth, positive change and organizational growth, engagement and agility, and a commonly understood direction which is frequently fueled by innovation.

The Three C's

To be truly effective, leaders must embrace and model the behaviors proven to gain *connection*, encourage *cooperation*, and enable *collaboration*. Specifically this means:
- Achieving connection by building trusting and collaborative relationships
- Gaining cooperation by positively influencing others
- Leading change by fostering the collaboration necessary to accomplish results

Part Three of LEAD will give you the tools to develop the three C's.

The Survey Says . . .

Recently, Dale Carnegie Training conducted an online survey of more than 3,300 full-time employees from a cross section of industries, company size, and positions in the organization—from individual contributors to CEOs—across fourteen representative countries from around the world. The primary objective of this cross-cultural leadership study was to identify key leadership characteristics that motivate and inspire people in the US and globally.

The survey required respondents to select positive leadership characteristics most likely to inspire and motivate them to do their best work. Employees were also asked which of their immediate supervisor's leadership behaviors are most important, and to rate the performance of their supervisor on those behaviors. Respondents also told us to what extent they could rely on their leaders to be honest with themselves and others, and finally, they reported their level of satisfaction with their job and their plans for staying with their current employer.

While some differences existed across countries and regions, the data reveals a remarkable number of similarities in the way employees think about their leaders—and leadership characteristics in general—which is useful for all of us to consider as we lead others.

When it comes to leadership behaviors essential to *engaging employees*, four high-level findings emerged from the study:

1. Leaders must give their employees sincere praise and appreciation.

It can get lost in the day-to-day rush to meet the next project deadline or delivery schedule, but simple, sincere appreciation, praise, and recognition are essential to motivating employees around the world. Once again, the data backs up what Dale Carnegie shared eighty years ago. That to be a leader, we should "Begin with praise and honest appreciation" (principle #22). Why? Eighty-five percent of respondents worldwide said that getting sincere appreciation from their supervisor was somewhat or very important to their desire to give their best work. More than three quarters (76%) said a leader who gives praise and honest appreciation would be more likely to inspire them, than someone who is more focused on getting the job done. It's especially important in the US and Canada, where employees tend to be particularly motivated by praise and appreciation compared with counterparts in other areas of the world.

What it means for us: Giving a continuous supply of well-founded, honest praise and sincere appreciation is the fuel your people need to keep running. Or as Mr. Carnegie said, "Praise the slightest improvement and praise every improvement. Be "hearty in your approbation and lavish in your praise" (principle #27).

2. Leaders do well to admit when they are wrong.
Everyone gets it wrong sometimes. That's life, and making mistakes is part of it. How we handle situations in which we realize we're wrong says volumes about what kind of person we are. It takes high levels of honesty, integrity, and courage to admit when we're wrong. Perhaps that's why so few leaders admit being wrong, despite Dale Carnegie's principle #12, which advises us that, "If you are wrong, admit it quickly and emphatically." More than eight in ten respondents worldwide (81%) said that having a leader who will admit when he or she is wrong is important or very important to inspiring them to give their best efforts at work. Admitting when we are wrong demonstrates that the environment is safe for taking calculated risks, making mistakes, and then learning from them. It creates an environment of "psychological safety," or one in which team

members feel safe to take risks in front of each other, which is shown to create high performing teams. And while good leaders usually make the right calls, even the best will undoubtedly have opportunities to prove their reliability, trustworthiness, and integrity by owning their mistakes.

What it means for us: Don't waste energy trying to cover up errors or mistakes. This only makes things worse. When we are wrong we should admit it, apologize for it (as needed), correct it, learn from it, and be a role model for others in how we respond to mistakes.

3. Effective leaders truly listen, and respect and value their employees' opinions.

People want to contribute to the mission and make a difference; that can only happen when leaders listen. Without it employees are left feeling disconnected and rejected. Dale Carnegie advised us to "Be a good listener. Encourage others to talk about themselves" (principle #7). Two of the top three leadership behaviors employees most often identified in the study as vital to their motivation were being "truly listened to" and "having their opinion respected" by their leader. Which is why Dale Carnegie's principle #25 advises us to "Ask questions instead of giving direct orders." The opportunities for direct and frequent communication between employers and their employees have never been more abundant given the available technology. Used wisely, leaders who listen can have tremendous impact. Henry David Thoreau wrote, "The greatest compliment that was ever paid me was when one asked me what I thought, and attended to my answer."

What it means for us: As leaders, we must remember that old cliche that we have one mouth and two ears, which means we should listen at least twice as much as we talk. Never underestimate the powerful effect of listening on our ability to lead effectively.

4. Employees want leaders they can trust to be honest with themselves *and* others.

The study examined trust in two ways, described as external and internal reliability. ***Externally reliable*** refers to leaders who are dependable, do what they say, and say what they do—people can count on them. Overall, only about thirty percent of respondents said their immediate supervisor can always be depended upon to be honest and trustworthy when dealing with others. Compared to Asia or Europe, respondents from North and South America were more likely to say their immediate supervisor is always honest. But with two-thirds of respondents saying they can't depend upon their manager to be honest, there is still work we need to do!

Leaders who are ***internally reliable*** demonstrate consistency in their beliefs and actions. They are true to themselves and avoid behaving in ways that are contrary to their core principles and beliefs. Again, only thirty percent of employees from around the world said their supervisor can *always* be trusted to say and do things consistent with their beliefs, with North and South America showing more leaders viewed positively in this regard compared with Asia and Europe.

What it means for us: Trust is the foundation of every relationship. Leaders who understand that it's based on more than just telling the truth when asked are on the right road to creating a culture that engages employees. In other words, we must commit to doing what we believe is right, and to living up to our commitments to motivate our people. It's not always easy to do, but leadership is not easy.

7. TRUST AND PERSONAL GROWTH

Warren couldn't help but glance at the clock on the wall again. It was 3:30 and Carl had promised to get those job descriptions in by the end of the day today. He'd followed the advice Fran gave him and had brought Carl in for an Innerview and then went through the feedback process and it seemed like Carl was on board. But, given how many times he'd delegated this task to Carl and not gotten results, Warren wasn't sure. He needed to be able to trust Carl to do the job, do it right, and honor his commitment to making today's deadline. Opening his work email for probably the twentieth time this afternoon, Warren checked to see if he'd gotten any messages from Carl.

Trust

In our experience, issues with trust fall into three broad areas: Character, Competence, and Commitment. Let's look a little more deeply at each.

Character

This relates to the external reliability we mentioned earlier. It's the first thing that comes to mind when we think of a "trust issue." This is a matter of honesty and integrity. It's doing the right thing when no one is looking. Not lying or cheating. More than that, it's the internal reliability, where we are doing what we know is the right thing to do, even when it is difficult or unpopular.

Linda is Armando's direct boss and they are traveling to a conference together. The company has given them an expense account to use for the trip. The conference is in the town where Linda grew up, and several of her friends and family come to see her while she's in town.

If Armando sees Linda using the account for non-business related items, such as personal shopping or taking friends to dinner and calling it a "business meeting," he is likely to lose trust in Linda as a leader. He knows that padding an expense account is dishonest, cheating, and is not the right thing to do, even though he knows that other people do it. Observing his boss doing these things causes dissonance for Armando, and he feels conflict between his own value system and what he's being shown by his leader. Even if she says, "Everyone does it," he doesn't agree with the practice and it reflects poorly on the company as a whole. If you're an honest person and you're working for a company where "everyone" cheats, what does that say? Even if it is only "one glass of wine with a friend," once there is evidence that someone can't be trusted, then doubts show up in other areas.

Conversely, let's say that Linda is scrupulously honest, and when her family comes to visit, he observes her using her own credit card for their expenses and keeping close track of legitimate business expenses, he can gather that Linda—and the company she represents as a leader—are trustworthy. This is the foundation of trust that is critical when we are placing our success and careers in the hands of our leaders.

Gaweed El Nakeeb, the Dale Carnegie trainer in Egypt, puts it this way. "This is one of the reasons why so many people love Dale Carnegie Training. We have strong standards when it comes to trainers applying principles. For example, integrity. Every trainer has to apply integrity both inside and outside the classroom. It always challenges you to personally apply what we train."

As leaders it is critically important for us to "walk our talk." If we say one thing yet do something else people see through that very quickly. Unless we live what we say, we are the wrong kind of role models for our teams. If we don't have integrity, we create rot that spreads through the organization based on our actions.

Competence

The second area where leaders can lose trust is in the area of competence. There are few things more discouraging than a boss who doesn't know the job. The leader doesn't necessarily have to be the best performer—in fact it's better than he or she isn't, since leading and doing are very different things—but he or she does have to have a core sense of the job requirements. If you're in the military and are in charge of a group of pilots, you pretty much need to know how to fly a plane.

Often there are competence gaps when the growth rate of a company or group is rapid. If you're working in a company with one product and it suddenly expands to five products, it takes time for competence—and trust in competence—to catch up.

In the scenario above, when a company expands rapidly, senior level leaders are often brought in to head the new divisions, or people are promoted quickly up the ranks. This, then, highlights development gaps in the team, where some people didn't grow at the same pace as others. People who were a good fit when the company was smaller don't always have the experience or skills to handle the complicated decisions that need to be made as a company grows. This leads to competence-based trust issues, as the senior leaders don't feel that some of the junior leaders can handle the job. They stop delegating, begin micromanaging, and reversing some decisions that have previously been made. The focus of the company becomes torn, as more time and effort is spent managing people and less on forward direction as a company.

As part of her development track rotation, Aika was placed in charge of a sales team. It was no secret that she hadn't been a salesperson in the organization. Yes, she had sold sneakers one summer when she was in university, but selling to businesses was another thing entirely. So she made it a big part of her first three months on the job to engage in "ride-along" sales calls a couple of days a week with the members of her team. She paid attention, asked lots of questions about their approach, and learned about how the process worked first hand. This also created the opportunity for Aika to have "Innerview" conversations with her team, and for her team to realize that while sales was a new area for her, Aika was a wealth of knowledge from other areas, including product management and marketing. These efforts not only helped her learn what her team was up against so that she could support them, but also created a solid foundation of trust for the working relationship.

Commitment

Finally, the third area of trust is that of commitment, or loyalty. This relates to both the leader feeling loyalty from his or her followers, and the follower feeling that his or her leader is loyal to them.

Until a few decades ago, the concept of workplace loyalty was practically a given. You started your career with a company, did your job diligently for forty years, and retired with a gold watch and a pension. That was what the world was like.

Things have of course changed since then, and few people have a linear career like that anymore. The concept of loyalty has changed. No longer can a boss tell someone to do something "because I said so" and expect compliance and loyalty. And, even if an employee does "all the right things," he or she can no longer expect an implied guarantee of employment, a lesson which historic numbers of people learned or re-learned during the COVID-19 pandemic.

The Importance of Trust

Simon was excited. It was his first day on the register at his new job at the dollar store. He'd been looking for a job for months and finally landed this one. He'd gone through online training and a very rushed onboarding program where he "shadowed" a couple of other employees for a short time. Most of them didn't speak English as their primary language and he wasn't sure he was ready to handle being on register alone. But his manager, Sue, gave him the assignment so he must be ready, right?

Sue was actually the regional manager who'd been acting as store manager while they filled a vacancy. Staffing had been an issue at this store, and people kept quitting. When Simon interviewed, she was just happy to have a good applicant and had hired him on the spot.

At the end of one shift, when they closed out Simon's register, he was $212 off. Simon started to panic! That was more than he had earned in the whole week he had been working there.

This was a moment of truth in Sue's leadership. All of the other employees were watching to see how she would handle it. Was it possible that Simon took the money? Was it an honest mistake?

Sue demanded that Simon follow her back out to the register, and announced to the other employees as they were walking, "Simon's register is $212 under. Just so you all know, this is a fireable offense." None of the other employees were making eye contact, but instead kept their heads down.

"Reach your hand in there, Simon and feel around to see if there are any loose bills."

Simon did and was relieved to find two $100 bills. "Whew!" he said as they went back to Sue's office to recount the money. "It's a lot better to be $12 short than $212!"

Sue turned back to him and said, "Not really, Simon. Our policy is that if you are more than $5 under, it's a disciplinary matter."

What message did Sue send as a leader? There are many levels of failure in this incident, but perhaps the worst is the demonstration of a lack of trust in Simon and not seeing the incident as an opportunity for growth for him or the team. Her attitude led Simon to quit the next day, and is likely part of why it was so hard to keep employees.

From this example we see how important trust is as an outcome of effective leadership. When we develop ourselves as a leader by role modeling the qualities we want to see in our direct reports and then apply the Human Relations Principles, tools and processes we've explored so far in the book, we develop reciprocal trust. When we don't, the trust isn't there. Without trust, leadership fails.

Another important outcome is that of Personal Growth. When we demonstrate effective leadership, both we and our direct reports have an opportunity to grow as people.

Personal Growth

"Hi, Marty, my name is Jenny and I'm the health educator and coach who your company hired to work with you all to achieve your health goals. A lot of companies these days are realizing the link between individual employee wellness and the overall success of the company. So, tell me what your biggest challenge is relating to your health."

Marty wasn't sure about this whole health coaching thing. It seemed like just another way for the company to pretend like they cared without having to address the real issues, but he decided to go along with it.

"Honestly, Jenny, it's my energy level. I am a dad with three young kids and a wife who stays at home with them. We just bought a townhouse and while there isn't a lot of yard work or anything like that, my wife has a lot of jobs for me on the weekend that she can't do herself. So between working forty-plus hours a week here, along with a commute, and then soccer games and house chores and a wife that wants some time with me too . . . it's just too much. I don't get enough sleep, let alone have time to eat right or exercise or do anything to take care of myself."

Jenny smiled and said, "Thanks for sharing that with me. I'm glad that you mentioned how challenging it can be to focus on your own needs and personal development. The best companies—the ones where employees love to work and where they stay the longest—are the ones who focus on the personal growth and development of their people."

While we may not be in a position to implement company-wide health coaching, we can create a culture of personal development in our direct reports.

Spending time, money, and other resources on the kinds of personal growth initiatives that aren't directly related to a person's job goes a long way in establishing the kind of trust that creates loyalty.

Nine Steps to Personal Growth

As a leader, there are nine steps you can use with your direct reports to help them grow. This is the Dale Carnegie Innovation Process, and it is based on The Osborn-Parnes Creative Problem-Solving Process—a structured way to generate creative and innovative ways to address problems.

1. Visualization: Picturing the "should be" ideal future.
2. Fact Finding: Determining the "as is" by gathering data about the current state.
3. Problem Finding: Identifying and prioritizing problems or opportunities.
4. Idea Finding: Green Light Thinking for ideas (brainstorming).
5. Solution Finding: Red Light Thinking to determine the best solution or approach.
6. Acceptance Finding: Gaining approval and support from others.
7. Implementation: Putting solutions into action (execution).
8. Follow Up: Monitoring Implementation.
9. Evaluation: Identifying and assessing end results.

In the case of Marty, he works with Jenny and goes through the nine steps.

1. Visualization: Picturing the "should be" ideal future.

"It would be great if I had enough energy for everything in my life. This includes exercise, eating right, spending quality time with my wife and kids, getting my house chores done and being effective at work."

2. Fact Finding: Determining the "as is" by gathering data about the current state.

In the next week, Marty goes through and identifies the current state of things. He talks to his wife, his kids, his coworkers, his boss, and looks at his current energy level in the various areas of life. He spends time tracking how he is actually spending his time, and makes note of all the activities that happen in his household. He writes it all down to meet with Jenny.

3. Problem Finding: Identifying and prioritizing problems or opportunities.

Working with Jenny, Marty looks at where the problems and opportunities lie. They identify things like the lack of a place to exercise, unhealthy food options at work, where the kids play soccer, spending too much time on weekend chores, and no alone time with his wife doing things that energize them both. He ends up working on the challenge of "How can I have more healthy habits at work?"

4. Idea Finding: Green Light Thinking for ideas (brainstorming).

Marty and Jenny use Green Light Thinking to brainstorm ideas. They come up with ideas like working out in his office, taking a gym lunch break, buying a microwave for his office to reheat healthy foods, getting a standing desk, getting a treadmill desk, parking farther from the door, always taking the stairs, and more. During the next week, he talks to his friends and colleagues and asks them about what they do, to add to his list. He writes down every idea, even the ones he thinks are a bit crazy.

5. Solution Finding: Red Light Thinking to determine the best solution or approach.

In his next meeting with Jenny they apply Red Light Thinking to select the best solutions. They decide to eliminate working out in his office and getting a microwave there, since he feels he needs to get out of the office. He swears off fast food and vending machine lunches. And he takes his wife's suggestion that he plan some time playing racquetball with his friends while she takes the kids to soccer; with the trade-off that then he can take care of the kids while she goes to have her own "me time."

6. Acceptance Finding: Gaining approval and support.

Marty talks to his team and tells them that he's going to be taking a lunch break every day to get in a workout and eat a healthy lunch. He asks that they not bother him with calls or messages unless it's an emergency. He asks them to help support him and remind him of his commitment. They are happy to hear he's taking better care of himself and they agree. He and his wife plan to make a schedule each Sunday night to align when he will play racquetball and when she can take her "me time."

7. Implementation: Putting solutions into action (execution).
For the next month, Marty puts the solutions into action. It's not always easy or perfect, but with support and reminders from his team, he succeeds much more often than when he gets caught up in work and skips his workout. When he next meets with Jenny she is shocked at how great he looks. He's lost a few pounds, but more than that he seems alert and energized.

8. Follow Up: Monitoring Implementation.
To keep things on track, Marty has a weekly call with Jenny to see how the implementation is going. When one of his team's projects was behind schedule and when his wife got sick, for example, he had to make some modifications to the plan, but he was able to work through each situation to make more healthy choices than he would have otherwise.

9. Evaluation: Identifying and assessing end results.
Two months later Jenny and Marty meet again to talk about how it's going. They assess the end result of the program that they initiated months ago, and discover that Marty is reporting feeling much more energy than he had before, and that he's committed to maintaining the approach which now feels like part of his daily routine.

This nine-step process is useful for working through any type of challenging situation and was developed based on what people naturally do when they are solving problems or creating opportunities successfully. When we use this process, we experience personal growth, both for ourselves as problem-solvers, leaders, and coaches, and also for the people who we lead. This happens whether it is through the direct interaction with our people, or by how we role model behavior that is appropriate in challenging situations. If we want to feel secure, we can stay in our comfort zones. But if we want to grow as leaders, we need to go outside of our comfort zones and stretch. This means a temporary loss of security. In other words, whenever we don't quite know what we are doing, we should know that we are growing and becoming an even better leader. And that is an important outcome.

In this chapter, we've talked about how Trust and Personal Growth are important components of leadership. In the next chapter, we'll talk about the second of the four outcomes: Positive Change and Organizational Growth.

Key Takeaways

- Issues with trust fall into three broad areas: Character, Competence, and Commitment.
- Character is a matter of honesty and integrity. It's doing the right thing when no one is looking. Not lying or cheating.
- Competence is having a core sense of what the jobs of one's direct reports entail as well as having core leadership skills.
- Commitment relates to both the leader feeling loyalty from his or her followers, and the follower feeling that his or her leader is loyal to them.
- The Dale Carnegie Innovation Process involves nine steps to personal growth. They are:
    1. Visualization: Picturing the "should be" ideal future.
    2. Fact Finding: Determining the "as is" by gathering data about the current state.
    3. Problem Finding: Identifying and prioritizing problems or opportunities.
    4. Idea Finding: Green Light Thinking for ideas (brainstorming).
    5. Solution Finding: Red Light Thinking to determine the best solution or approach.
    6. Acceptance Finding: Gaining approval and support.
    7. Implementation: Putting solutions into action (execution).
    8. Follow Up: Monitoring Implementation.
    9. Evaluation: Identifying and assessing end results.

8. POSITIVE CHANGE AND ORGANIZATIONAL GROWTH

The year was 2006 and iconic automaker Ford Motor Company was struggling. The name that had once been synonymous with "cool muscle cars" like the Mustang—and breakthrough development processes like for the first Ford Taurus—was caught up in the economic turmoil that led to the automotive industry government bailout.

Ford had a secret weapon that allowed it to be the one US automobile company that turned itself around without taking any of the taxpayer's bailout money. That secret weapon was newly minted CEO Alan Mulally.

During the years Mulally was at the helm of Ford, the company went from a $5.8 billion *quarterly* loss—and headed for bankruptcy—to generating billions in profits each year; starting in 2009 through well after his departure in 2014. Even though the numbers have been trending downward the past few years, the recovery from almost bankrupt to enviable profit during the Great Recession—without declaring bankruptcy or receiving a government bailout, all while actively changing the culture of an organization—is remarkable.

How did Mulally do it? Through effective leadership and a deep understanding of the principles of how people—and companies—react to change. He boils it down to two words: "Working together." It may sound simple, but it is not easy.

Great leaders must be masters of change management. This is true at every level of the organization, from first line managers to C-suite executives.

But leading change can be difficult, and it's complicated by another trend in the workplace: work groups and cross-functional teams that are spread over miles, across time zones and even international borders. Without real face-to-face interaction and strong cultural awareness it can be even more challenging for leaders at every level to create alignment, maintain accountability, and achieve objectives.

Mulally knew this better than anyone. With an organization that spanned the globe, a diverse product line, and a multinational workforce, it was a challenge to understand the entire company as a whole. In addition to Ford, there was Ford of Europe, Ford of Asia and a host of other divisions and subsidiaries including Volvo, Jaguar and Aston Martin. And there was little coordination, or even cooperation between—and within—its many parts.

The first step in managing the change was to bring these disparate regional divisions together into a single, global enterprise.

Forbes Magazine explains it this way. "'What I've learned is the power of a compelling vision,' [Mulally said]. Mulally's first priority was to craft a vision the entire company could rally behind. It had to be bold, compelling, actionable, and concise. Mulally understood the power of simplicity. Mulally crafted a two-word vision . . . that he called, 'One Ford.' One Ford has several components, such as consolidating, unifying, and simplifying Ford's global operations. Those two words—One Ford—were part of Mulally's everyday conversations, meetings, interviews, and emails. He even carried the words with him on a laminated card. One automobile analyst said Mulally's vision was 'precisely what the troops needed—a clear direction.*'"

According to *Fast Company*, in an early meeting with reporters, Mulally was asked if he was interested in a merger. "Yes!" he exclaimed with a big grin as the reporters all whipped open their notebooks. "We're going to merge with ourselves."**

Embracing Change

Embracing change is at the heart of Dale Carnegie's philosophy for success. As are the interpersonal skills required to build the trusted work relationships and psychologically-safe working environments that support innovation and make implementing change easier.

---

* https://www.forbes.com/sites/carminegallo/2014/05/16/steve-jobs-and-alan-mulally-unleashed-innovation-with-two-simple-words/#7d54ac0e6275

** https://www.fastcompany.com/1680075/saving-an-iconic-brand-five-ways-alan-mulally-changed-ford-s-culture

Leaders are responsible for the communication of that desired vision. Keep in mind that just because leaders and managers within an organization understand the need for change, that doesn't mean their direct reports, peers, or even bosses do too.

People need to be convinced that the change has value and is worth embracing. Dramatizing the vision of the post-change state and explaining how the change will enable the organization to more fully deliver on its purpose will help. Dale Carnegie tells us to "Dramatize our ideas," in Principle #20. By this he means to give attention to communicating the need for change in a way that connects it to the organization's purpose, appeals to employees' motives, and makes the change objective clear and creates accountability. Don't give them facts or drone on with a bunch of buzzwords; create something vivid and dramatic that people can see and feel. When we do this, we're paying attention to The People Side of Change.

The People Side of Change

As we mentioned, *LEAD!* is an action-oriented book that's designed to help you apply what you're learning. To that end, take the following quiz to test your understanding about "the people side of change." Answer true or false for the following questions.

1. Our response to change is based in part on the way change is managed.
2. If we've experienced a lot of change recently we may react to change more negatively than usual.

3. Our feelings about change can be avoided.
4. The larger the scope of the change, the longer it may take for us to accept or support it.
5. Some people respond positively to every change.
6. If our feelings about a change are acknowledged by the change leader, we're more likely to trust that person.
7. A primary reason people resist a given change is that the vision is not clear.
8. If people are involved in every stage of a change they will move more quickly to acceptance and support.
9. Effective change leadership balances people, process, and organizational focus.
10. Clearly communicating why and how the current state is deficient (prompting the need for change) supports moving from resistance to acceptance.
11. A common reason change fails is not enough effort is devoted to managing the people aspect of the change.
12. If a change is well planned and managed it will succeed.

Let's take a look at the answers.

1. Our response to change is based in part on the way change is managed. TRUE. Our reaction to the change is shaped by how the change is managed and implemented, and this has more of an impact than the simple fact of the change itself.
2. If we've experienced a lot of change recently we may react to change more negatively than usual. TRUE.

The more change we experience, the more stressful it is for us as humans, and eventually we start to rebel against the change just because of our fatigue from all the changes.

3. Our feelings about change can be avoided. FALSE. While our reactions can be managed, our emotions cannot be avoided. Even if we don't show them, we still feel them.
4. The larger the scope of the change, the longer it may take for us to accept or support it. TRUE. Simply put, it is easier for us to get on board with small changes than major changes.
5. Some people respond positively to every change. FALSE. Even people whose innate tendency is to embrace change or view things in a positive light may struggle with some changes.
6. If our feelings about a change are acknowledged by the change leader, we're more likely to trust that person. TRUE. When people demonstrate sympathy and empathy, we know that they are working to understand our perspective, which helps to build trust.
7. A primary reason people resist a given change is that the vision is not clear. TRUE. It is difficult for people to embrace the destination if they don't understand what it is, how they'll get there, why it is important, or perhaps most importantly, what it means for them.
8. If people are involved in every stage of a change they will move more quickly to acceptance and support. FALSE. If the change is complex, if there has been a

good deal of recent change, or if the change moves them outside of their comfort zone, they may resist change even when actively involved.
9. Effective change leadership balances people, process, and organizational focus. TRUE. As leaders, we can't just look at any of these three ingredients in isolation. We must look at all of these items to increase the likelihood of success.
10. Clearly communicating why and how the current state is deficient (prompting the need for change) supports moving from resistance to acceptance. TRUE. In the words of Dale Carnegie, "Arouse in the other person an eager want" for the future state, so that they can see why they should leave behind what is currently true (principle #3).
11. A common reason change fails is not enough effort is devoted to managing the people aspect of the change. TRUE. So many change management efforts focus on the change itself, and not on the impact of the change on the people, which is why people resist the change. So the efforts fail.
12. If a change is well planned and managed it will succeed. FALSE. Some changes are poor ideas in the first place, some are good ideas implemented at the wrong time, and others are being done for the wrong reason.

If some of the answers surprised you, read on to learn more about the people side of change and how to apply it to your leadership.

Reactions to Change

People's reaction to the idea of change varies. Some people will embrace it, immediately seeing the potential upside. Others will reject it, no matter how logical the need for change is. Most of the time, people's emotional reactions range from passive to active and change over time and across individuals. Here are some of the common emotional reactions to change.

- **Shock**: A sort of mental paralysis when first facing the prospect of change. When we are in "shock" we may have trouble processing/remembering information.
- **Denial**: When initial shock wears off it is replaced with a sense of disbelief and hope that the change won't really happen.
- **Anger**: As the disbelief fades and evidence that the change will actually happen erodes denial, a sense of anger may set in.
- **Bargaining**: As anger recedes, people facing change may try negotiating the terms of the change, including their role, the scope, and the process.
- **Dejection**: Dejection may set in when, even after sharing concerns and trying to bargain, people realize not everything they asked for has been agreed to.
- **Letting Go**: As the realities of the change become clearer, people experience a letting go of what they'd been holding onto (current state and hopes they can either stop or modify the change).
- **Exploration**: After letting go, people begin to "explore" the realities of the change and test out what the future state will be like.

- **Acceptance**: After exploring, people have a clearer vision of the change and expectations and begin to accept and even be eager for the change.

Not everyone reacts to changes consistently, and different people will react to the same change in different ways. Yet we all move through these stages, and at different rates. You may only spend a fraction of a second in some phases of the process and yet spend two weeks in another phase.

As an example, imagine your boss were to tell you that your pay is going to double starting at the end of next month. It may feel like you immediately and joyfully jump to "Acceptance," yet you would no doubt initially be shocked and wonder if it were true or if this were merely a cruel prank. You might even be angry that she hadn't done it sooner, or tried to bargain to make it effective at the end of this month. Maybe you're dejected that your boss didn't triple it, but likely you'd let go of the old salary, start thinking about how you might spend your newly found wealth, and then be eager for your next paycheck. No matter how long it takes to get to acceptance, you go through all of the stages before you arrive at the end point.

Explore how you'd feel if you were to find out that your pay will be cut in half starting at the end of next month. Could you envision shock? Denial? Anger? Bargaining? Dejection? Letting go? Exploration? And eventual Acceptance? Likely it would take you longer to accept this change. Or you may avoid the change altogether by leaving the company. That's always a possibility.

It's clear that recognizing these responses and managing the change process is important for leaders at every level so that they can make sure that the change is as positive as possible. However, the success or failure of change can often be heavily influenced by senior leadership and its approach to change and growth.

Dale Carnegie Trainer Gaweed El Nakeeb puts it this way. "When we are leading teams, it is important—crucially important—to look for how we *disagree* rather than how we *agree*. How we disagree when it comes to making changes makes the difference, even if we have rules or processes set (majority rule, for example). The mechanism of making the decision doesn't mean that people won't feel sour or angry if they're opposed to the change." Said another way, don't expect the bull not to charge you, just because you're a vegetarian.

At Dale Carnegie Training we teach a planning process that helps leaders to prevent these kinds of problems. Whether it's an organizational change, like a hamburger chain adopting a vegetarian hamburger, or at the team level executing a project, the following eight step planning process is effective at preventing problems.

Planning Process

1. Desired outcome
2. Current situation
3. Goals
4. Action Steps
5. Time Frames

6. Resources
7. Obstacles and Contingencies
8. Tracking and Measurement

1. By starting with the **desired outcome** first, the leader (or leaders) is able to clarify a vision for the future. This is where effective storytelling can come in. When a leader can create an emotionally impactful story that gets the leader involved, they can more effectively envision the desired outcome.

Elizabeth Haberberger, President of Dale Carnegie St. Louis, shares a story about an emerging leader who discovered this power.

> The HR director at a manufacturing company took a Dale Carnegie leadership course. During the course, she, as well as everyone else in the class, had to share with the group a moment that defined her as a leader. Before the presentations, everyone had a chance to gather their thoughts and practice with a partner. Just before she stood up to speak in front of the class she realized that, "my defining moment isn't this. I need to tell the real defining moment." Instead of what she had planned to say, she stood up and spoke from her heart. The entire class was captivated and was profoundly moved! Her presentation was so impactful and heartwarming that she won the Outstanding Performance Award for the class, despite her lack of practice! Her response? "I never knew I could move people emotionally until that presentation. Now I can use this as a leader in Human Resources."

2. Next, look at the **current situation**. In the case with Marty and the health coaching, he took some time to assess where things are. In the case of Burger King, before launching the Impossible (vegetarian) Whopper, their sales were lagging far behind their competitors, and they could see the data that more and more people were reducing their meat consumption and looking for a tasty alternative.

3. Setting **goals** is the next step. As we mentioned earlier, goals need to be attainable, and this often means taking bigger goals and breaking them down into smaller ones, which can then be delegated to subject matter experts. If Marty had decided he needed to lose forty pounds, or decrease his bad cholesterol level by thirty points, that may have seemed like a huge insurmountable challenge. However, by focusing on lunch breaks and soccer games, it felt more manageable.

4. From goals come **action steps**. This happens throughout the organization, from top leadership down to front line employees. Everyone needs to know exactly what they have to do to accomplish the goals. For Marty, it meant that he committed to working out during lunch, and eating a healthy lunch (rather than unhealthy fast food), and playing racquetball during his childrens' soccer practices.

5. This leads to **time frames**. When will the action steps be completed to achieve the goals. In the case of Warren Cantel, he learned that he needed to be even more specific about when each deliverable needed to be completed, rather than

just having expectations that others may or may not have met. As leaders we need to be clear about "X by Y," in other words, what specifically needs to be done, and by when.

6. Do the team members have the **resources** they need? From funding to supplies, in order to achieve a goal, one needs the resources to do so. In the case of Burger King, they needed to be assured that the supply problem that Impossible Foods faced earlier in the year was solved before they committed to rolling out the Impossible Whopper nationwide. Would they have the resources they needed? If you're asking your team members to adapt a new sales management software system, do they have access to the internet outside of their office? On their phones? Can their technology handle the new system? Is training and support available for them? Does it communicate with other systems? Ensure that you have figured out the total cost for the entire plan and that you take into account the costs of people, material, and time before you execute.

7. While identifying **obstacles and contingencies** is never perfect, it's important to have as clear an idea of the obstacles that could come up as possible. This is where a classic business SWOT analysis can come in handy. When you identify your company's internal **S**trengths and **W**eaknesses, as well as the external **O**pportunities, and **T**hreats, you're better able to see obstacles and then determine how you might overcome them. In the case of Burger King, recognizing that their competitors had access to a viable competitor was a serious obstacle they needed to address if

they were to provide a unique offering—and the accompanying sales increases on which they planned. Understanding the obstacles is important, as is understanding what contingency plans we'll implement if we encounter those obstacles. Build into the plan what to do if something bad happens, and we're more likely to overcome the obstacles.

8. Finally, with any goal, we need to have a system in place for **tracking and measurement**. In the case of Marty in the previous chapter, they measured his success in terms of self-perceived energy level, and could have tracked it based on the number of racquetball games and workouts per week. For Burger King, tracking things like store visits, sales of the new product, repeat purchases and average customer purchase amounts will allow them to see the success and areas for growth with their change initiative.

Bottom line is that we can't leave change to chance. It's important to be deliberate about building our plans using the planning process. Taking time to ensure successful execution is a wise investment in our success. As leaders we cannot create the levels of change and growth that our organizations need to achieve their goals, without thinking about the people and the processes.

In the next chapter, we'll discuss another outcome of effective leadership: Employee Engagement and Agility.

Key Takeaways

- If we stay in our comfort zone, we will not grow as leaders
- Embracing change means that people need to be convinced that the change has value and is worth embracing.
- To do this, leaders should focus as much on the people side of change as they do on the logistical side of it.
- When people encounter a change, they experience these emotions, which cannot be avoided:
    - Shock
    - Denial
    - Anger
    - Bargaining
    - Dejection
    - Letting go
    - Exploration
    - Acceptance
- Dale Carnegie's Planning Process is:
    1. Desired outcome
    2. Current situation
    3. Goals
    4. Action Steps
    5. Time Frames
    6. Resources
    7. Obstacles and Contingencies
    8. Tracking and Measurement

9. ENGAGEMENT AND AGILITY

"Warren, it's great to see you again." Fran was amazed at the difference in Warren Cantel's appearance. He literally looked different. It was clear that the leadership training she'd given him had paid off. His posture was taller and he had a confident air about him that had been missing before.

"You too, Fran. Is that a new picture of your family?" Warren noticed a newly framed photo on her desk, and Fran told him that it had been taken on a weekend hiking trip in the mountains. As she did, Warren pulled out the chair opposite Fran's desk and sat down. In the few short months since he'd been in here initially, he'd managed to transform his team's morale.

"So Warren, how are things going?"

"Really well, Fran. As you know, my issues with Carl were resolved a few weeks ago and he delivered

the job descriptions on time, which we used at the hiring fair we held. Got a few really good candidates that we're interviewing. Leah and Carl are heading up the interviews and actually they're excited about it!"

"I'm impressed at how you've embraced your leadership role, Warren."

He smiled sincerely at the compliment. "Well, it's a good team. But you already know that."

She did. What had been a fragmented and disjointed group was transformed into an engaged, cohesive team. As Warren described the various relationships between the people on the team, Fran smiled, knowing that she'd been right to promote Warren. All he needed was some training and to use the principles she'd learned so long ago.

How did Warren and Fran create such engaged employees? By establishing a "people first" culture, as Alan Mullaly called it.

Employee Engagement

Employee Engagement is defined as a feeling of commitment, passion, and energy which translates to:
- High levels of effort
- Persistence with even the most difficult tasks
- A collaborative work environment
- Employees committed to working to achieve results

Engaged employees are involved in the decisions that affect them, and believe that their leaders have a sincere interest in employee well being. The organization operates with honesty and integrity, and there is clarity on how the leader's role supports the organization's success. They also have adequate resources to get the job done right.

Employee engagement is relevant at every level of leadership. At Dale Carnegie Training we've identified an Engagement Continuum that ranges from Disengaged to Engaged with steps in between. The more engaged an employee is, the harder they'll work, the happier they'll be, and the longer they'll stay working for the company. From a results perspective, the more engaged they are, the more effective they'll be for you.

Imagine that you're playing tug of war. Your team is on your side. At the other end of the rope is one of the organizations against which you compete in the marketplace. Those people on your team that are engaged fully will be pulling with every ounce of strength they've got. The compliant ones may be leaning back to apply their weight to the rope. The indifferent ones are likely just standing there, and if we're lucky, they have their hands on the rope. And the Disengaged ones are probably pushing the rope towards the competitors! In order to win this game, we know who we want on our team (and who we want on the competitor's team)!

Engagement Continuum

Disengaged   Indifferent   Compliant   Engaged

◄─────────────────────────────────────►

Influencers of Engagement

What are some of the things that influence employee engagement? A lot of it has to do with the things we've covered in this book. When a leader is a role model, gives employees the tools he or she needs to do the job, pairs it with personal growth opportunities and recognition and reward, engagement increases. Here are the key areas that we've found influence engagement:

- Relationship with Supervisor
- Goals and objectives are clear
- Leaders care about how employees feel
- Employes feel empowered

People First Culture

To accomplish this, the organization should develop a "people first" culture. Based on Alan Mulally's approach, we describe it this way:

Everyone knows the plan + Everyone knows the status of the plan + Everyone knows the areas that require special attention = profitable and/or successful growth for all.

Google founders Larry Page and Sergey Brin put it this way: "We have somewhat of a social mission, and most other companies do not. I think that's why people like working for us and using our services . . . Companies' goals should be to make their employees so wealthy that they do not need to work, but choose to because they believe in the company. Hopefully, I believe in a world of abundance, and in that world, many of our employees don't have to work, they're pretty wealthy, they could probably go years without working. Why are they working? They're working because they like doing something, they believe in what they're doing."

Organizational Agility

In order to accomplish this and create a company filled with engaged employees, the leaders have to set the stage for organizational agility. Agility requires an openness to new information and learning, a positive attitude toward change, and confidence that it can succeed.

There are many things that can inhibit an organization's ability to be agile: bureaucracy that slows down processes, internal politics that prolong decision-making, silos that hide the root causes of problems and ownership of solutions, and a lack of trust that makes communication difficult, to name just a few. When these barriers to agility exist, the fix isn't simple, but neither is it insurmountable.

Unless we're near the top of the organization chart, we have less control and influence about what goes on across the organization. But when we develop a culture within our team that encourages open communication and empowers people to come up with new ways of doing things, we're encouraging agility.

Leaders at every level need to gather and act on information, make decisions quickly, and implement change to meet rapidly evolving requirements of customers and the business environment. No matter at which level of the organization we reside, that ability to adapt and shift helps the organization be more agile.

Relationships Are At The Heart of Agility

The foundations for agility are at the heart of Dale Carnegie's approach to relationships and the interpersonal skills he began teaching decades ago.

> *Agility involves seeking out new information and embracing continuous change in a collaborative way.*

Efficient tools and processes that make use of the advantages today's technology offers, along with accurate data, are essential. Organizations need to proactively ask the right questions, gather, share, and analyze information—the impetus for change—and then make decisions and act. The Innovation Process that we shared in chapter seven helps us to do this more effectively and efficiently.

But no amount of data will help you become agile if there's no genuine desire to listen to what the data says. And those who lack confidence often lack the courage to truly listen. That's why *it takes more than smart people and good data to become agile*. Along with good tools and processes, it takes the right combination of being able to bounce back from a setback (resiliency), ability to understand and work with others (social intelligence), and capacity for action, aligned with a clear organizational purpose, to create a strong foundation for agility.

Agile leaders expect to operate in an environment where the path forward isn't set in stone; it's understood that new information may prompt a course adjustment at any time. A customer-centered purpose is the compass that allows employees to continue to navigate toward the ultimate objective, even as the path takes unexpected turns. A clear focus on creating value for the customer provides a true north for everyone, and supports agility in several ways.

First, it provides the reason for change: to fulfill the purpose more fully by *meeting customer needs more efficiently and effectively.* This, in turn, empowers engaged employees to suggest changes that will increase responsiveness in providing value for customers. Purpose also helps connect employees with their customers, and customers have increasingly become a good source of intellectual capital for co-creation of value.

For example, during the Great Recession of the late 2000s, when car sales were suffering, Hyundai realized that people weren't buying new cars because they were scared of losing their jobs. So they created the innovative Assurance Job Loss Protection program that helped it gain significant market share and grow into a mainstream US brand. The program allowed new car buyers to return their car if they lost their job, which helped allay the fear of buyers during an economic crisis. Hyundai later adapted this program during the economic downturn that accompanied the COVID-19 pandemic in 2020.*

Second, having a shared goal (the customer-centered purpose) that is actually considered before functional metrics *helps break down silos and also helps people work through conflict.* When disagreements arise over strategy and tactics, a shared commitment to delivering on purpose can help keep people in dialogue, working together toward a solution. When competing priorities threaten to complicate the decision-making process, a customer-centered purpose provides people with a reliable way to assess their relative importance, make trade-off decisions, and then explain those decisions to others with confidence.

As an example, a cosmetics company developed a persona of their typical customer based on who regularly purchased their products, and named her "Kate." They developed a rich description of her life, her attitudes and what she needed, and shared it throughout the organization. They had pictures of this imaginary person in their meeting rooms, and when there was a debate, they would ask, "what would Kate want?" This helped teams create better solutions based on the customer needs.

---

* https://www.forbes.com/sites/dalebuss/2020/03/31/hyundai-reprises-assurance-program-for-coronavirus-era/#26c3a60a1951

Finally, having a customer-centered purpose to which employees can connect their achievements *helps each person see the value of what they do.* This purpose-driven work increases engagement—and engaged employees help make organizations more agile. When the direction is clear, empowered people will naturally create new and improved ways to get there in the fastest way possible.

Li, one leader of a product development team, was focused on making the customer's lives better so they could change their organizations and the world, and he sought to encourage the team by talking about changing the world. Yet through a team conversation, Li discovered that this wasn't necessarily the most important thing for each member of the team. The purposes of each individual included creating something cool, recognition, accomplishment, making a difference, working with a good team, and more. So Li had a series of individual conversations to understand the purpose of each individual, and then kept a list of team members and what motivated them. Li referenced it before conversations with them so that he could help them see their work through the lens of their purpose, rather than his own. This helped to stoke the fire of commitment in each individual member of his team.

Engaged Employees are Agile

Agile leaders have the ability to change in response to insights on the evolving requirements of customers and the business environment—and they do it quickly, without provoking resistance or resentment among employees.

New information is the impetus for change, but Dale Carnegie research shows that only thirty percent of survey respondents strongly agree that their organization has the capacity to act in response to change. Imagine the missed opportunities for growth for the other seventy percent of companies. Dale Carnegie once advised us to, "Keep your mind open to change all the time. It is only by examining and reexamining your opinions and ideas that you can progress." This is the heart of agility for an individual, and for all of the individuals that make up an organization.

Enhancing an organization's capacity for action involves supporting the collaboration and creative intelligence that drives innovation, and effectively leading continuous change. Without the ability to work together to explore and develop new solutions, we are limited by what we can do alone. The goal is to encourage a productive "creative abrasion" where individual ideas can rub up against others and spark even more innovative solutions. This is the value of the Thinking Mechanism that we discussed in Part 1.

Agility requires an openness to new information and learning, a positive attitude toward change, and confidence that it can succeed. It thrives in an environment of trust and psychological safety, where people are empowered, engaged, and connected to a customer-centered purpose. And it requires an effective set of tools, processes, creative and social intelligence, and competent change leadership.

Agile leaders free people to experiment, adapt, and innovate. As the pace of change accelerates and gains momentum, these imperatives have become higher profile, but in reality, they've always been part of the attributes that put people and companies ahead. Certainly there is much more freedom in start up organizations, which is why they tend to be much more agile, and why established organizations with processes, infrastructure, bureaucracy, and structure tend to be slower and more rigid. However, don't let this dissuade you from working to be agile or instilling agility in your team. Recognize the boundaries in which you must work, and those which you can step beyond in order to engage people and create innovation.

In this chapter, we talked about how creating an engaged workforce allows an organization to become agile. In the next chapter, we'll bring it all together and discuss planning a common direction.

Key Takeaways

- Employee Engagement is defined as a feeling of commitment, passion, and energy which translates to high levels of effort, persistence with even the most difficult tasks, a collaborative work environment, and employees committed to working to achieve results.
- The engagement continuum ranges from Disengaged, to Indifferent, to Compliant, to Engaged.
- Some influencers of engagement are: Relationship with Supervisor, Goals and objectives are clear, Leaders care about how employees feel, Employees are empowered.
- Engaged employees are agile. Along with good tools and processes, it takes the right combination of resilience, social intelligence and capacity for action, aligned with a clear organizational purpose, to create a strong foundation for agility.
- A people first culture is one where Everyone knows the plan + Everyone knows the status of the plan + Everyone knows the areas that require special attention, and this leads to profitable and/or successful growth for all.
- When you develop a culture within your team that encourages open communication and empowers people to come up with new ways of doing things, you're encouraging agility, which results in innovation.

10. COMMON DIRECTION AND INNOVATION

Robin and Barry have been watching the construction for weeks. A new Five Guys Burgers and Fries franchise is just about to open in their neighborhood, and they're excited to try it. Five Guys, a restaurant in the "better burger" category of hamburger restaurants, is slated to become a key competitor of In-n-Out Burgers in their town. In fact, it's overtaken the regional chain to become the number one burger franchise in its category. Since Robin and Barry love In-n-Out, they're eagerly awaiting Five Guys' opening day.

The big day finally arrives. Robin and Barry walk in and notice the red and white checkered decor. There are signs all around with testimonials from Five Guys' customers in other cities. The kitchen is open and Robin and Barry can see the cooks busily filling orders. The menu is simple, with only burgers, fries, and hot dogs. But, with free toppings like cheeses, bacon, grilled vegetables and onions, sauces, and cajun seasoning for the fries, Five Guys boasts that there are more than 250,000 ways to order a burger. They even have vegetarian options, with cheese only or grilled vegetables. Five Guys also offers free in-shell peanuts to snack on while diners are waiting for their orders to be ready.

Five Guys' History

Five Guys Burgers and Fries opened in Virginia in 1986 as a local family business. It was started by Jerry Murrell when his two oldest sons were about to graduate high school and told him that they weren't interested in going to college. Jerry agreed, on one condition. He would take the money they'd saved for tuition and open a family business. The company was named after Jerry and his (then) four sons, Jim, Matt, Chad, and Ben. When the family had a fifth son, Tyler, Jerry considered him the "fifth" guy.

Each son has a different role in the company. Jim helps manage the whole operation, Matt opens new locations, Chad does manager training, Ben handles IT, and Tyler manages relationships with vendors. At first, the sons ran the business while Jerry kept his "day job." Once the business took off, he quit his job and now runs the business with his sons. They all play to their strengths and their interests which helps them be successful leaders.

Five Guys leads what's known as the "better burger" category (hamburgers in the $8 range) of fast-casual restaurants, a $2.2 billion segment that grew sixteen percent in 2013. (Five Guys represented nearly half of the segment.)

The entire burger category is a $40 billion industry in the US, dominated by McDonald's, Burger King and Wendy's. Growth there has been slower (3.2% last year). But, Ronald and the King don't need to worry. They're competing for different customers. The audience of diners who visit fast food burger joints are more price and speed conscious than quality conscious. In other words, you don't go to a fast food place to get high quality ingredients. You go there to get your food cheap and fast.

By offering better quality, more expensive burgers, and defining themselves as "fast casual," Five Guys is choosing a different playing field; one that plays to their strengths and their interests. That's an important distinction for any leader. How you lead depends on the game you're playing.

Just as we mentioned earlier that a football team's offensive leaders have to develop a different method than their defensive ones, and that Phil Jackson had to lead Kobe differently than he did Shaq, the individual leaders at the different Five Guys franchises have to lead differently than each other. They have to be true to themselves and to the people and the communities in which they lead. A Five Guys in an upscale community in California is likely to have different kinds of employees than a Five Guys in a more urban environment. While the actual management (i.e. processes related to the work) of employees is likely to be standardized from corporate, the way to lead the restaurant is dependent on context. How can a leader energize, engage, and connect with his or her direct reports? The answer is going to be different depending on the makeup of the employees and the situation in which we're leading. And while we may need to lead people in different ways, one thing that keeps the team together is a common direction.

Planning a Common Direction

Melanie received a frantic phone call from her son, Robert. Her husband, Paul, was in the hospital with a broken ankle. Robert told her to come to the hospital near the gym right away, and to bring their insurance information. She also needed to make sure that the decisions that needed to be made regarding surgical options to repair Paul's destroyed ankle weren't being influenced either by his pain or the painkillers he was on. She knew the climbing gym where Paul and Robert had been working out when the accident occurred, so she drove to the hospital, which was halfway between her home and the gym. As she was walking into the hospital, she asked Robert where they were. Robert said he would walk her to the ER unit once she got to the front door. Stephanie informed Robert that she was at the front door, but he couldn't see her. Turns out that the ambulance had taken Paul to a different hospital that was closer to the gym which was farther from their home, but Stephanie didn't know that. Once they figured out the error, Stephanie jumped in her car and drove to the other hospital.

Unfortunately, this type of error happens frequently with teams. A team will be working on a project, and people will be going about it in different ways, which end up causing confusion, frustration, delays, and rework, because while everyone may have been moving in a direction, it wasn't the same direction.

When leaders are effective, a key outcome is a direction that is understood by all. This requires the leader to both create the direction (ideally with the team), and then ensure that everyone is on-board and committed to it. It seems simple enough, but it is frequently overlooked in the rush to get things done. Two key elements of getting everyone on-board and committed to a common direction are the Team Purpose Statement and the Strategic Plan.

Team Purpose Statement: A description of why we exist. It inspires us, directs our actions, and guides our decisions. It is the reason why we are working on the team or the project.

A purpose statement should be . . .
1. Brief
2. Repeatable (easy to remember)
3. Unique (versus generic)
4. Have an emotional impact (a reflection of the values of the organization/team)

To create this with your team, do some Green Light Thinking about the "why" or the team or project's reason for being. Dig deeper into this question to get beyond the obvious "to build a new gizmo." Explore why that gizmo is important, explore what it brings to the customer, the organization, and the world. Each time someone suggests a purpose, ask "why is that important?" When you ask this question enough, you eventually get to an answer that's something like, "to create a wonderful world!" That's a pretty good indication that you've expanded it enough. Once you've completed your Green Light Thinking, do some careful Red Light Thinking to explore which of the statements get the team fired up. That fourth criteria, "Have an emotional impact," can make the difference between a ho-hum project and/or team and something that creates excitement and enthusiasm. Apple founder Steve Jobs' purpose wasn't to invent computers and phones, it was to "put a ding in the universe." While he was an imperfect leader to be sure, his ability to inspire employees and customers with his purpose changed the way we live and interact with each other.

Strategic Plan Outputs: Employees who understand the connection between the organization's purpose, goals, and results are more likely to take appropriate actions without being told what to do every moment because they understand how their actions affect results.

Walk into most offices or businesses and you'll probably see a "mission statement" or a "company vision" on the wall somewhere. In many cases these dusty plaques were created by committed leaders who were trying to do the right thing. Unfortunately, often the mission/vision statement is completed, rolled out with great fanfare, engraved on a piece of brass, hung on the wall of the lobby and promptly forgotten as people "get back to work."

While libraries full of books have been written about strategic planning, and people will debate the differences between a mission statement and a vision for hours, we won't get into that argument here. What is important is that the answers to "why do we exist (purpose)" and "where are we going (vision)" are important yet by themselves insufficient in ensuring your team knows where they are going. You probably learned about strategic planning, or your organization has a strategic planning process, and you should use that, as long as it incorporates the necessary elements.

Ensure that your strategic plan has items like the ones below to align goals and communicate with your team on how they will be monitored and measured. It is important that the Strategic Plan's purpose aligns with the organization's vision and values. From there you can work through the process of setting goals for your team and get the results you are desiring by setting clear measurables for employees. And this is where the magic happens. When the activities and measures line up with the "why" and the "where we're going," it ensures that the team is aligned and headed in the same direction. This also allows the leader to ensure that the team is doing the right things the right way by keeping track of those activities according to the measurements.

An Example

A large clothing manufacturer created their innovation strategy to share with the organization. They were able to condense the plan to two key words: "go outside." They weren't just telling people to take a walk, they were asking everyone in the organization to look for new ideas outside of their normal experiences by exploring. "Go outside" meant that everyone should talk to other people, look at other industries, look at what consumers were doing. In other words, the employees were being asked to leave their cubicle or conference room, get their noses out of their computers, assembly lines, or sewing machines and to search for other ways of doing things or creating new products. These two words applied to everyone in the organization whether they were the CEO or sewing underwear. Based on these two words and the organization's values, each individual leader was asked to create a strategy for their division, department, and team, that would demonstrate how they would "go outside." From this strategy, teams would create their activities (e.g. "talk to consumers") and define measurements for the activity (e.g. "ask two consumers per week what they like and don't like about their shoes").

Common direction doesn't need to be complicated. Ideally it should be something that people can understand, and something that gets them emotionally involved in the work, so that the plan is more than a list of annoying tasks to do. It should also be something that gets everyone excited about going in the same direction.

Innovation Drives Change

The final area where effective leadership shows at an organizational level is Innovation. The Innovation-Change Cycle is such that change drives the need for innovation, and then innovation fuels further change.

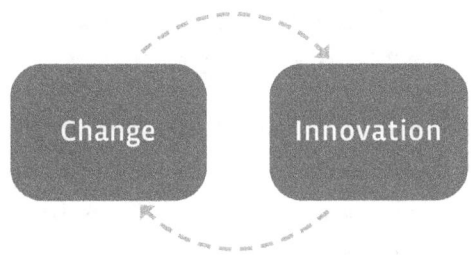

In order to understand how innovation drives change, it's useful to look at Kurt Lewin's approach to change management known as Force Field Analysis.* In the model, two types of forces are examined: those that promote change and those that resist change. The forces that promote change are called *driving forces* and those that attempt to maintain the status quo are called *restraining forces* or *resisting forces*. According to the model, in order for any change to occur, the driving forces must exceed the restraining forces, thus upsetting the balance.

How does this apply to us as leaders? When a leader creates a culture of innovation and resists the urge to say "but this is how we've always done things," then the team looks for ways to improve and create new and improved solutions.

---

* Lewin, K. (1946). Force field analysis. *The 1973 Annual Handbook for Group Facilitators*, 111-13.

> *By empowering your workers to try a different approach, new solutions can be discovered, and that's what leads to growth.*

Disruptive Innovation For Emerging Leaders

One doesn't have to be a CTO to develop a technology that disrupts the status quo. Ben Pate was an instructor at a martial arts studio in 2006 and was frustrated with the difficulty of scheduling and managing clients. An avid coder with a degree in computer science, Ben created a client management platform to help his studio run more efficiently. Soon, other studios began requesting the platform and eventually Pate and his wife formed the company Zen Planner. Zen Planner is used at thousands of studios and Crossfit boxes across the United States.

Despite the media hype, to become an innovator you don't need to disrupt your whole industry. You just need to focus on building relationships with your key customers and empower your team to find innovative ways to serve them better.

> *Every innovation doesn't have to be disruptive. The world needs both disruptive and adaptive change/innovation*

Are You An Improver or a Disruptor?

The truth is, there is no one right reaction to change. We all have different preferences. Take the following assessment to determine your Change Orientation.

Place a checkmark next to the one descriptor in each row that you think well describes you when you are facing change. Be honest to get a more accurate assessment. Then, add up the number of checkmarks in each column and place that number in the Total row.

1	Prefer change to the status quo		Prefer change that is gradual or incremental	
2	Enjoy taking risks		Follow the rules	
3	Prefer solutions that break all the rules		Prefer tested, proven solutions	
4	Enjoy spontaneity		Enjoy predictability	
5	Work spontaneously and non-sequentially		Work in a precise and methodical way	
6	Comfortable challenging the current state		Comfortable with tradition	
7	Seek to test structure, rules, and norms		Seek stability	
8	Advocate for individuality		Advocate for collaboration	
9	Want far-reaching change		Want structure	
	Total:		Total:	

The change orientation is best expressed as a continuum, with changes and people falling on the continuum.

Disrupters — — — — — — — — — — **Improvers**

In the assessment above, if the column on the left has more checks, you prefer to be more of a disrupter. If there are more checks in the right column, your preference is to be more of an improver. If the number of checkmarks are similar, that puts you more in the middle of the continuum.

Most people are not at either end of the continuum and are somewhere in between the two extremes. And most people tend to lean towards one end of the continuum or the other. Where you are on the continuum compared to the people you work with may have an impact on how you work together.

People towards the "Disrupter" side of the continuum can visualize the "big picture," can serve as advocates for needed change, are creative thinkers or visionaries, and are able to reorganize systems by re-creating them.

People towards the "Improver" end of the spectrum encourage analysis, serve as the repository for "history," can serve to slow down the change process so effective decisions can be made, expect cooperation, and tend to be more practical.

Understanding that one is not right and the other wrong is important, even when it feels that way to us. Despite the hype, innovation does not occur only because of disrupters, nor does it occur only because of improvers. Look at any successful innovation and you'll see a combination of the two. The microwave oven was a disruptive idea when it was invented, and the first ones were about the size of a large refrigerator. Only with constant improvements were they made safer, smaller, less expensive, and so useful for reheating food that they are in most kitchens today. Airbnb certainly disrupted the lodging business. But it wouldn't be as successful without the hundreds and hundreds of improvements in the way that the company operates—in the app, the business model, government regulations, the expansion from city-to-city, partnerships, marketing, service extensions, and so on—to get it to the point where the service is easy to use and wildly popular.

Know that wherever you are on the continuum, you have a valuable role to play in innovation. And this is true for everyone on your team. Your challenge as a leader is to figure out how to get the right balance of disruption and improvement to achieve your team's purpose and innovation goals.

Innovation is Never "Complete"

An important idea is the concept that innovation is never something that's "finished." In order to stay fresh and relevant, innovation has to be constant. This doesn't mean that we change things just for the sake of changing them. Instead, we need to have systems in place to create a culture of innovation, and not just at the organization level. Innovation needs to happen throughout the company. Even if you're not the Chief Innovation Officer, you can lead innovation efforts that can create change.

Jonathan Vehar tells the story of three administrative assistants who were working in a department with a culture that was so negative that employees could not wait to be transferred to another group. But these three admins didn't have this luxury. . . . they were stuck. So they decided to change the situation. They used the Innovation Process to assess their situation, determine the problem, generate solutions, and then implemented a pretty simple plan. Each of these three regularly found themselves with their colleagues as part of a conversation at their desks . . . it was a natural gathering place since there were no walls to their cubicles. These conversations inevitably turned to complaints by the colleagues about the team, the work, the leader, the culture, etc. As gently as they could, at some point in the conversation the admins would ask the simple question, "So what are you going to do about it?" They didn't ask it as an angry challenge, but as a gentle, suggestive inquiry. This simple question shifted the tone of the conversation from whining and complaining, and enabled people to create a different way of working, being and leading. In fact, these three admins were role modelling the behaviors they wanted the entire department to take on. And they were successful. Over time, the culture improved, the turnover slowed, and morale improved. Notice that it did not require an intervention by the Chief Culture Officer, the Chief Innovation Officer, the Chief Talent Officer or the Chief Executive Officer. No chief was involved. Only three people who decided to take responsibility to lead people to a different way of working.

The Dale Carnegie Innovation Process

The steps of the Dale Carnegie Innovation Process should, by now, be starting to look familiar. They are the same steps we've covered in the personal and organizational change processes. After all, what is innovation but finding a new solution to a pressing problem? Leading innovation is about leading people into and through change.

Here are the steps again:
1. Visualization: Picturing the "should be" ideal future
2. Fact Finding: Determining the "as is" by gathering data about the current state
3. Problem Finding: Identifying and prioritizing problems or opportunities
4. Idea Finding: Green Light Thinking for ideas (brainstorming)
5. Solution Finding: Red Light Thinking to determine the best solution or approach
6. Acceptance Finding: Gaining approval and support
7. Implementation: Putting solutions into action (execution)
8. Follow Up: Monitoring Implementation
9. Evaluation: Identifying and assessing end results

To use this process, it's a matter of connecting with your key customers and walking them through the first few steps. Find out what they want from your company as an ideal. Determine the current state. Discover what the problems and opportunities are. Brainstorm solutions. Implement them, and see how they work. The process works whether the "customer" is an internal stakeholder or an external end user. And it's effective whether you're the Chief Innovation Officer, a department head, or an administrative assistant in an unpleasant culture.

In this chapter, we provided approaches to show how effective leaders establish a common direction that allows for innovative solutions to problems.

Key Takeaways

- The ability to plan projects, both large and small, simple and complicated, is essential in today's business environment.
- Two ways to get everyone on-board and committed to a common direction are the Team Purpose Statement and the Strategic Plan Outputs.
- A Team Purpose Statement should be Brief, Repeatable, Unique, and Have an emotional impact.
- Successful project management involves the following steps: Should Be, As Is, Goals, Action Steps, Cost, Timetables, Implementation, Follow Up/Measurement.
- An important idea is the concept that innovation is never something that's "finished." In order to stay fresh and relevant, innovation has to be constant.
- The Innovation-Change Cycle is such that change drives innovation, and then innovation fuels further change.
- There is no one right reaction to change.
- Leading innovation is about leading people into and through change.
- To become an innovator, you don't need to disrupt your whole industry. You just need to focus on building relationships with your key customers and empower your team to find innovative ways to serve them better.

CONCLUSION
Your Desired Performance Results

Dale Carnegie Model of Leadership Success

As we look at the Dale Carnegie Model of Leadership Success again, we can see how far we've come. From how to behave, to what to do, and the outcomes that emerge, we've explored several different approaches and techniques to take your leadership to the next level. And throughout, a key message of *LEAD!* is that the timeless principles that were taught by Dale Carnegie so many years ago still apply. After all, no matter how technology changes and societal norms evolve, people are still people.

So while all of the boxes on the left hand side of the model are important, without results, they're only nice to have. And while it's possible to achieve short-term results by ignoring all of the boxes on the left and being a tyrannical leader, for sustained results that maximize the output from the people in the organization, we need to work hard to develop our role modelling, our application of the Human Relations Principles, and the tools and process, as well as paying attention to the outcomes. Great leaders pay attention to all of the items in the model, not with the goal of being liked or creating a culture that's "nice," but with the goal of creating outstanding results that benefit everyone in the organization, whether they're shareholders, customers, or employees. We believe that everyone wants to contribute to something great, and by achieving results we enable people to fulfill their true potential.

Underneath the Leadership Success Model is a simple premise that we work on every day at Dale Carnegie: we believe that everyone has inherent greatness. And we also believe that it is the job of leaders to see and unlock that greatness in the people we are privileged to lead. Nothing more, nothing less. That opportunity is a trust that has been granted to those of us who lead, whether that is our formal role due to our title and position in the organization chart, or because we serve as an informal leader to whom people look for guidance based on our actions, and that trust is fragile. Yet it is with this opportunity that we can positively change lives, organizations, communities, and even the world. Imagine the legacy you can leave when you take on this responsibility.

> *"There are so many different lenses to view your world. There's the people lens, the profit lens, the efficiency lens, and the customer lens. As long as you have your people lens on first, you are going to make good decisions."*
> —Elizabeth Haberberger, President, Dale Carnegie Training of St. Louis

Looking Ahead

Top performing organizations know that effective leadership is not a luxury; it is essential to their success.

Leaders shape the culture. Effective leaders recognize their actions may have both intended and unintended consequences, so they carefully consider the culture that their actions will help shape. They recognize that by creating a positive climate that inspires team members, they influence them to contribute their best.

Leaders are committed to developing their people and helping people uncover their blind spots. Great leaders are fully committed to the success of their people and are willing to invest time and energy in them. They intuitively see potential and know how to bring out the best in them. They realize that only by bringing out the greatness in their team members can their team demonstrate high potential.

Leaders build and maintain productive relationships. Leadership is not a solitary activity, nor is the focus on the leader; rather it is about how leaders treat the people with whom they work and how they make people feel about themselves and the work. This allows leaders to influence and be influenced by others to achieve the best possible results. To get things done with and through other people, leaders must demonstrate that they genuinely care about the people with whom they work. This is what inspires team members to go above and beyond.

Leaders need to give people the self-confidence to be the best version of themselves. People would rather work for someone who builds them up rather than putting them down. They must treat others well and with respect. In many cases, people don't quit jobs, they quit leaders, especially the leaders that don't seem to care about them and aren't committed to their growth.

Why This Makes a Difference

We often promote our top-performing employees into leadership positions, assuming they can immediately transform into an effective leader. The fact is that the skillset and mindset are completely different and require different competencies. Organizations face two challenges: losing the work output from the employee's prior role, while gaining a leader who is learning on the job.

Once a new leader has mastered the basics, how do they develop their team to reach their full potential and meet organizational goals? How do they guide them through periods of change? How do they become innovative leaders?

Leadership is about relationships. Dale Carnegie's unique relationship-centered approach to leadership development provides you with a comprehensive toolkit that will help you become the type of leader required in today's workforce. This book combines the crucially important hard skills and proven behaviors that leaders need, while also focusing on adopting the right attitudes required to be an engaging leader.

Consider this book your next step in a life-long development effort to be even more effective. And as a next step, we'd invite you to join Dale Carnegie's leadership training that targets specific stages of a leader's development and the skills needed to be successful at each stage.

- Since leadership is about relationships with people, only Dale Carnegie courses are based on the proven Dale Carnegie Human Relations Principles that are timeless, universal, and guide everything we do.
- We provide practical skills that can be applied immediately, not just theories, buzzwords, fads or "flavors of the month."
- We recognize that being a leader means being responsible for more than just yourself, and that is stressful. That's why we provide practices to help reduce stress and worry.
- Our work is based on the wisdom and expertise gained from developing leaders longer than anyone else doing this work.

- Rather than trying to have people be someone they're not, we help people bring out their greatness—their authentic self and inner leader.
- We provide expertise from the organization that literally wrote the book on influence and building relationships.
- Leaders can't and shouldn't try to do it all on their own. We deliver the knowledge and skills to help leaders accomplish work with and through others.

We invite you to find out more at DaleCarnegie.com

A Path to Leadership Development

Research shows that organizations need and are seeking leaders with competencies to handle the variety of challenges they face in today's business environment. Specific competencies gain importance depending on where the leader is in his or her development:

- High-potential team members being considered for leadership need to develop and exhibit the self-confidence and interpersonal skills that will be essential for success in their new roles.
- New leaders need help transitioning from doing the work themselves to leading their team. Competencies at this stage of leadership development include using authority appropriately, being self-directed, developing others, and holding people accountable.
- Experienced leaders achieve success for the organization by working to bring out the greatness in their people.

They do this by focusing on "next level" competencies that address the types of challenges they face in their roles: leading people through change, delegation that helps develop the people on their teams, innovation, and more.

No matter your leadership experience or at what level you are in your company—from a front line manager to a CEO—the elements of the Dale Carnegie Leadership Success Model will help you become a better leader and allow you to better solve the problems that matter to you. What matters most is how you use the principles taught here to achieve your own desired results. What kind of leader do you want to be? Be intentional about it, and be that leader as of right now. We believe there is no time like the present to start being that leader. We know you have the potential to become a great leader because everyone does in their own unique way. We wish you every success on your leadership journey.

"Knowledge isn't power until it is applied."
—DALE CARNEGIE

INDEX

A

absentee leadership, 118–119
acceptance finding
    in innovation process, 95, 219
    nature of, 171
    in personal growth, 171, 173
    as reaction to change, 185
accountability, 39–62
    competence in, 44, 45–47
    in decision making, 45, 56–61
    Framework for Handling Performance Deviations, 145–150
    goal accomplishment in, 44–45, 53–56
    honesty in, 44, 50–52
    integrity in, 41, 44, 50–52
    leadership tools and processes for, 131–135, 143–150
    moral courage in, 49–50
    as personal, 41–43
    positive feedback and, 135–144
    qualities of, 43–61
action steps, in the organizational planning process, 188
agility. *see* organizational agility
Airbnb, 50–52, 216–217
Amazon, 155
"Analysts" listener type
    communicating with, 73
    described, 71
    self-evaluation and, 75
anger, as reaction to change, 184
Apple, 210
appreciation, importance of, 34, 158–159
Armstrong, Neil, 114
aspirational leaders, 2
authority, in strategic leadership, 91

B

bargaining, as reaction to change, 184
Bezos, Jeff, 155–156
Bianco, Fran (case)
  accountability and, 39–41
  applying Human Relations Principles, 103–104
  employee engagement and, 193–194
  leadership tools and processes and, 123–128
  "others focus" and, 63–64
  self-awareness and, 21–23
  strategic leadership and, 87–88
blind spots
  identifying, 34–36, 77
  self-awareness vs., 26–28, 34–36
Blockbuster, 54
brainstorming
  in innovation process, 93, 94, 127
  in personal growth, 172–173
Brin, Sergey, 197
British Journal of Management, 118
Bryant, Kobe, 116–117, 207
Buffett, Warren, 46
Build Trust/Be a Friendlier Person principles, 105–108
  illustration of, 105–108
  in the Leadership Pyramid, 104
  overview, 17, 20, 108
Burger King, 188, 189–190, 207

C

Cantel, Warren (case)
  accountability and, 39–41
  applying Human Relations Principles, 103–104
  engagement and, 193–194
  leadership tools and processes and, 123–128, 142, 149–150
  "others focus" and, 63–64, 83–84
  self-awareness and, 21–23, 24, 28
  strategic leadership and, 87–88
  time frames for organizational planning process, 188–189
  trust and, 163
Cardiello, Joe
  on being a leader, 117
  "others focus" and, 81–82
Carlson, Chester, 44–45
Carnegie, Dale
  How to Win Friends and Influence People, 1, 6, 100, 104
  Human Relations Principles. *see* Human Relations Principles
  on knowledge as power, 227
  Leadership Success Model. *see* Dale Carnegie Model of Leadership Success
  on listening, 160
  on mistakes, 139
  people first culture and, 1–3

positive change and, 179–180
on praise and appreciation, 158–160
three C's and, 14, 157–162
causative questions, 134
change
change orientation and, 215–217
positive. *see* positive change
character, trust and, 164–165
Chilean mining accident (2010), 9–10, 12, 30
coaching
in the Dale Carnegie Coaching Process, 139–142
of effective leaders, 100
in the NBA (National Basketball Association), 80, 116–117, 207
collaboration, nature and importance of, 14, 157
Collins, Jim, 31
"Combatives" listener type
communicating with, 73
described, 70
self-evaluation and, 75
commitment
in strategic leadership, 88
trust and, 167–168
common direction, 205–220
change orientation and, 215–217
examples of, 205–208, 212
at Five Guys Burgers and Fries, 205–208
planning, 208–211
communication skills, 67–80

improving listening skills, 76–77
listener types and, 67–80
self-evaluation of listening skills, 74–75, 77–80
competence
in accountability, 44, 45–47
trust and, 165–167
connection, nature and importance of, 14, 157
consistency, integrity and, 47–49
cooperation, nature and importance of, 14, 157
COVID-19 pandemic, 12–13, 45, 117, 168, 200
current situation, in the organizational planning process, 188
customer-centered purpose, 199–201

D

Dale Carnegie Coaching Process, 139–142
Dale Carnegie Innovation Process, 171–175, 218–219
Dale Carnegie Leadership Storytelling Formula, 110–114, 124, 135
Dale Carnegie Model of Leadership Success
applications of, 19, 156
importance of effective leadership, 223–224
"others focus" and, 84
outcomes of, 19, 155–220

Dale Carnegie Model of Leadership Success (*cont.*)
  overview of, 15–16, 19, 99–101, 156. *see also* accountability; "others-focused" mindset; self-awareness; strategic leadership
  as path to leadership development, 15–16, 226–227
  role models in, 16, 23, 41, 63–85, 156
  timeless principles of, 221–223
  top-performing employees and, 224–227
decision making, accountability in, 45, 56–61
dejection, as reaction to change, 184
delegation process, 128–131
  process for delegation, 128–131
  reasons for delegation, 128
  task assignment vs., 130–131
denial, as reaction to change, 184
desired outcome, in the organizational planning process, 187
disruptive innovation, 214–217

E
Eastman Kodak, 54
Edison, Thomas, 90
El Nakeeb, Gaweed
  character and, 165
  positive change and, 186
  on self-underestimation, 30–31

empathy, of effective leaders, 2–3
employee engagement, 193–204
  defined, 194
  Engagement Continuum and, 195, 196
  influencers of, 196
  organizational agility and, 201–203
  in "others-focused" mindset, 80
  people first culture and, 196–197
  relationships at heart of, 198–201
engagement. *see* employee engagement
"Engagers" listener type
  communicating with, 73
  described, 71
  self-evaluation and, 75
Escher, Herb, accountability and, 45
evaluation. *see also* self-evaluation
  in innovation process, 95–96, 219
  nature of, 171
Ewers, Kim, people first culture and, 6
exploration, as reaction to change, 184
external reliability, 161, 164–165

F
Facebook, 66, 80–81, 155
fact finding
  in innovation process, 93, 219
  nature of, 171
  in personal growth, 171, 172
factual questions, 133

Fast Company, 179
feedback
positive. *see* positive feedback
in 360-degree feedback evaluation, 24, 25, 35, 39
Five Guys Burgers and Fries, 205–208
follow up
in innovation process, 95, 219
nature of, 171
in personal growth, 171, 174
Forbes magazine, 179
Force Field Analysis, 213
Ford Motor Company, 29–30, 91, 177–179, 196
forward focus, in strategic leadership, 89, 90–91
Framework for Handling Performance Deviations, 145–150
example of use, 149–150
steps in, 145–149

G

Gain Cooperation/Win People to Your Way of Thinking
principles, 109–115
illustration of, 109–110
in the Leadership Pyramid, 104
Leadership Storytelling Formula and, 110–114, 124, 135
manipulation vs., 115
overview, 17–18, 114–115
Galvin, Bob, accountability and, 60
GameStop, 53–54
General Electric, 99
gig economy, 50–52
goal setting/accomplishment
in accountability, 44–45, 53–56
in the Chilean mining accident (2010), 9–10
customer-centered purpose and, 200
GOALS steps in, 54–56
in the organizational planning process, 188
self-direction and, 29
Good to Great (Collins), 31
Google, 155, 197
GoPro, 57–58
Great Recession, 30, 177–178, 199–200
Green Light Thinking
in innovation process, 94
nature of, 94, 127
in personal growth, 172–173
in planning a common direction, 209–210
Gretzky, Wayne, 89
growth
organizational. *see* organizational growth
personal. *see* personal growth

H

Haberberger, Elizabeth
accountability and, 46, 47
blind spots vs. self-awareness and, 26–27
and desired change in the organizational planning process, 187
people first culture and, 223

Haloid/Xerox, 44–45
Hamilton, Lisa, "others focus" and, 66
Harley Davidson, 56–57
Hart, Joe, 1–3
honesty
    in accountability, 44, 50–52
    importance of, 161–162
How to Win Friends and Influence People (Carnegie), 1, 6, 100, 104
Huang, Laura, 109–110
Human Relations Principles, 3, 6, 14
    applying, 103–121
    Build Trust/Be a Friendlier Person, 17, 20, 104, 105–108
    Gain Cooperation/Win People to Your Way of Thinking, 17–18, 104, 109–115
    Lead Change/Be a Leader, 18, 104, 115–117
    Leadership Pyramid and, 104–117
    overview, 16–18
Hyundai, 199–200

I

idea finding
    in innovation process, 94, 219
    nature of, 171
    in personal growth, 171, 172–173
identity, reputation vs., 28–29
implementation
    in innovation process, 95, 219
    nature of, 171
    in personal growth, 171, 174
incompetent leadership, 118–119
influence
    power vs., 31–32, 92
    in strategic leadership, 92
Innerviews, 132–135
    goal of, 135
    power of, 132–133
    question types in, 133–134
innovation, 205–220
    change orientation and, 215–217
    Dale Carnegie Innovation Process and, 171–175, 218–219
    disruptive, for emerging leaders, 214–217
    in driving change, 213–219
    examples of, 205–208, 212
    fact-finding in, 93, 219
    Innovation-Change Cycle and, 213
    as never "complete," 217–218
    steps in, 92–96, 219
    in strategic leadership, 90, 92–96
integrity, 47–61
    in accountability, 41, 44, 50–52
    consistency and, 47–49
    honesty and, 50–52
    in managing progress toward goals, 53–56
    moral courage and, 49–50
    nature of, 50
internal reliability, 161, 164
"Interrupters" listener type

communicating with, 72
described, 70
self-evaluation and, 74

J
Jackson, Phil, 80, 116–117, 207
Japan Sales Mastery (Story), 76–77
Jha, Pallavi, on transition to leadership, 23–24
Jobs, Steve, 210
Johnson, Kevin, 49–50
Jordan, Michael, 116–117

K
Kakaur, Kent, performance accountability and, 131–132
Khosroshahi, Dara, 155–156
Kodak, 54

L
laissez-faire leadership, 118, 138
Lead Change/Be a Leader principles, 115–120
Framework for Handling Performance Deviations and, 145–150
illustrations of, 115–117
in the Leadership Pyramid, 104
overview, 18, 119
leadership. *see also* Dale Carnegie Model of Leadership Success; leadership tools and processes
becoming a leader, 15–16
characteristics of effective leaders, 2–3, 13–14
in the Chilean mining accident (2010), 9–10, 12, 30
designated, 12
importance of effective, 13, 223–224
incompetent, 118–119
influence vs. power and, 31–32, 92
leaders of influence vs. leaders of power, 31–32
management vs., 13
nature of, 12, 13–15
"others-focused" mindset and. *see* "others-focused" mindset
R.E.A.L. leaders, 2–3
situationally dependent, 12
strategic. *see* strategic leadership
transition to, 23–26, 27–28
types of, 118–119, 138
Leadership Pyramid, 104–117
Leadership Storytelling Formula, 110–114, 124, 135
Leadership Success Model. *see* Dale Carnegie Model of Leadership Success
leadership tools and processes, 123–152
Dale Carnegie Coaching Process, 139–142
Dale Carnegie Innovation Process, 171–175, 218–219
Dale Carnegie Leadership Storytelling Formula, 110–114, 124, 135

leadership tools and processes (*cont.*)
  delegation process, 128–131
  Framework for Handling Performance Deviations, 145–150
  Human Relations Principles. see Human Relations Principles
  Innerviews, 132–135
  Leadership Success Model. see Dale Carnegie Model of Leadership Success
  levels of positive feedback, 135–144
  performance accountability, 131–135, 143–150
  thinking mechanism and, 126–128, 202. *see also* Green Light Thinking; Red Light Thinking

Lean In (Sandberg), 66

learning
  by effective leaders, 2
  "learner's mind" and, 2, 36, 46

letting go, as reaction to change, 184

Lewin, Kurt, 213

listening skills, 67–80
  communication and listener types, 71–73
  identifying blind spots, 34–35, 77
  illustration of, 75–76
  importance of, 34–35, 71, 160–161
  improving, 76–77
  self-evaluation of, 74–75, 77–80
  types of listeners, 69–73

M

management, leadership vs., 13

Marone, Mark, "others focus" and, 82–83

McDonald's, 155, 207

Merrill, Clark
  "others focus" and, 64–65
  power of Innerview and, 132–133

Miller, Cynthia, transition to leadership, 24–25, 27–28

mistakes
  admitting, 34, 48, 52, 159–160
  discussing, 139
  margin of error and, 143

moral courage/ethics, in accountability, 49–50

Motorola, 60

Mulally, Alan, 29–30, 91, 177–179, 196

Murrell, Jerry, 206

Musk, Elon, 109–110

N

NBA (National Basketball Association), 80, 116–117, 207

Netflix, 54

Nooyi, Indra
  on developing others, 66, 91
  on self-development, 30

O

obstacles and contingencies, in the organizational planning process, 189–190
O'Neal, Shaquille, 116–117, 207
opportunity finding. *see* problem/opportunity finding
organizational agility, 197–203
    engaged employees and, 201–203
    inhibition of, 197
    nature of, 197
    relationships at heart of, 198–201
organizational growth. *see also* positive change
    at Ford Motor Company, 177–179
    planning process for, 186–190
organizational planning process
    common direction in, 208–211
    steps in, 186–190
Osborn-Parnes Creative Problem-Solving Process, 171
"others-focused" mindset, 63–85. *see also* people first culture
    change facilitation in, 80–81
    characteristics of, 65–84
    collaboration in, 80
    communication/listening skills in, 67–80
    developing others in, 66, 91
    employee engagement in, 80
    fostering teamwork in, 80
    inspiring others in, 65–66
    nature and importance of, 64
    positively influencing others in, 66–67
    providing direction in, 81–84
    service by leaders, 64–65
    uncovering employee hopes and dreams, 82–83
    working cooperatively in, 81
"Out-to-Lunchers" listener type
    communicating with, 72
    described, 70
    self-evaluation and, 74

P

Page, Larry, 197
Palm Pilot, 91
Pate, Ben, 214
peak performance, 142–143
people first culture. *see also* "others-focused" mindset
    Dale Carnegie and, 1–3
    customer-centered purpose and, 199–201
    employee engagement and, 196–197
    at Ford Motor Company, 29–30
    importance of, 223
    people side of change and, 180–183
Pepsico, 30, 66, 91
performance accountability. *see* accountability; Framework for Handling Performance Deviations

personal growth, 169–175
  accountability as personal and, 41–43
  nature of, 170–171
  steps to, 171–175
Pichai, Sundar, 155–156
Pilsner, Mark, transition to leadership, 25, 27–28
planning. *see* organizational planning process
positive change, 177–191
  change orientation and, 215–217
  customer-centered purpose and, 199–201
  embracing, 179–180
  at Ford Motor Company, 177–179
  Innovation-Change Cycle and, 213
  innovation in driving, 213–219
  in "others-focused" mindset, 80–81
  people side of change, 180–183
  planning process for, 186–190
  reactions to change, 184–186
positive feedback, 135–144
  coaching higher levels of performance, 139–142
  empty praise vs., 138
  examples of, 137–138
  levels of, 136
  margin of error and, 143
  peak performance and, 142–143
  subpar performance and, 143–144

power
  influence vs., 31–32, 92
  of Innerviews, 132–133
praise
  empty, 138
  importance of, 34, 158–159
"Preoccupied" listener type
  communicating with, 72
  described, 69
  self-evaluation and, 74
problem/opportunity finding
  accountability and, 56–57
  in innovation process, 93, 219
  nature of, 171
  in personal growth, 171, 172
problem solving/solution finding
  accountability and, 56–61
  in innovation process, 95, 219
  nature of, 171
  in personal growth, 171, 173
  in strategic leadership, 90

Q

question types, 133–134
  causative, 134
  factual, 133
  values-based, 134

R

racial bias training, 49–50
reading, importance of daily, 46
R.E.A.L. leaders, 2–3
Red Light Thinking
  in innovation process, 94
  nature of, 94, 127
  in personal growth, 173
  in planning a common direction, 209–210

reliability
    of effective leaders, 2
    external, 161, 164–165
    internal, 161, 164
reputation, identity vs., 28–29
resiliency, 199
resources, in the organizational planning process, 189
role models, 16, 23, 41, 156. *see also* "others-focused" mindset

S

Sandberg, Sheryl, 66
self-awareness, 21–37
    assessing level of, 33
    blind spots vs., 26–28, 34–36
    developing, 33–34
    leaders of influence vs. leaders of power, 31
    of personal listening type and skills, 74–75, 77–80
    qualities that determine, 29–30
    reputation vs. identity and, 28–29
    selfishness vs., 32
    360-degree feedback and, 24, 25, 35, 39
    underestimating self vs., 30–31
self-confidence, 30, 88
self-development, 30
self-direction, 29
self-evaluation
    of change orientation, 215–217
    of listener type, 74–76
    of listening skills, 77–80
    in personal growth, 171, 174
selfishness, 32
self-regulation, 29–30
shock, as reaction to change, 184
social intelligence, 199
solution finding. *see* problem solving/solution finding
SpaceX, 110
Starbucks, 49–50
Stewart, Doug, coaching effective leaders and, 100
Story, Greg
    on innovation process, 92–96
    "others focus" and, 76–77
storytelling
    Leadership Storytelling Formula and, 110–114, 124, 135
    in the organizational planning process, 187
strategic leadership, 87–97
    authority in, 91
    characteristics of, 89–91
    forward focus in, 89, 90–91
    innovation in, 90, 92–96
    nature of strategic leaders, 91–92
    problem solving in, 90
    seeing through the other side of the board, 88–89
    tameshiwari principles in, 88–89
Strickholm, Karen, accountability and, 60
Sugar Shack, 47–48
supportive disloyal leadership, 118
SWOT analysis, 189–190

T

tameshiwari principles, 88–89
task assignment, delegation vs., 130–131
teamwork
  collaboration and, 14, 157
  in "others-focused" mindset, 80
thinking mechanism, 126–128, 202. *see also* Green Light Thinking; Red Light Thinking
Thomas, Kelly, honesty and, 50–52
Thoreau, Henry David, 160
360-degree feedback evaluation, 24, 25, 35, 39
three C's
  applications of, 157–162
  nature and importance of, 14, 157
time frames, in the organizational planning process, 188–189
Tolstoy, Leo, 30–31
tracking and measurement, in the organizational planning process, 190
trust, 163–176. *see also* Build Trust/Be a Friendlier Person principles
  areas of, 164–168
  character and, 164–165
  commitment and, 167–168
  competence and, 165–167
  external reliability and, 161, 164–165
  honesty and, 161–162
  importance of, 3, 35, 76, 168–171
  internal reliability and, 161, 164
  personal growth and, 169–175
Turner, Ryan, 47–48
tyrannical leadership, 118

U

Uber, 155
underestimating self, 30–31
Urzua, Luis, 9–10, 12, 30

V

values-based questions, 134
Vehar, Jonathan
  innovation process and, 217–218
  self-awareness and, 33–34
  strategic leadership and, 90–91
visualization
  in innovation process, 93, 219
  nature of, 171
  in personal growth, 171, 172
Volkswagen, 44, 48

W

Walmart, 155
Welch, Jack, 99
Wendy's, 207
"Whatevers" listener type
  communicating with, 72–73
  described, 70
  self-evaluation and, 74

Z

Zen Planner, 214
Zinsmeister, Anita, accountability and, 42–43, 44
Zuckerberg, Mark, 155–156

CPSIA information can be obtained
at www.ICGtesting.com
Printed in the USA
JSHW040826090221
11597JS00002BB/4